Sheep

Sheep

Alan Butler

BOOKS

Winchester, U.K.
New York, U.S.A.

First published by O Books, 2006
An imprint of John Hunt Publishing Ltd.,
The Bothy, Deershot Lodge, Park Lane, Ropley,
Hants, SO24 0BE, UK
office@johnhunt-publishing.com
www.o-books.net

USA and Canada	Singapore
NBN	STP
custserv@nbnbooks.com	davidbuckland@tlp.com.sg
Tel: 1 800 462 6420	Tel: 65 6276
Fax: 1 800 338 4550	Fax: 65 6276 7119
Australia	**South Africa**
Brumby Books	Alternative Books
sales@brumbybooks.com	altbook@global.co.za
Tel: 61 3 9761 5535	Tel: 27 011 792 7730
Fax: 61 3 9761 7095	Fax: 27 011 972 7787

Design: Jim Weaver Design
Cover design: Book Design, London

ISBN-13: 978 1 905047 68 0
ISBN-10: 1 905047 68 1

A CIP catalogue record for this book is available from the
British Library.

Printed by Maple-Vail, USA

Contents

Introduction

There's no getting away from it – sheep inspire humour in people. I've lost count of the number of friends and associates who have either smiled politely or even burst out laughing when I told them I was currently working on a book that detailed the incredible importance of sheep in the building of the world we inhabit. Fortunately many of the same people stopped laughing when they read the draft copy of what follows in this book.

The fact is that the existence of sheep was not simply a significant component in creating today's world – their presence has represented a pivotal factor in not one or two but literally dozens of different ways. It seems strange that such an inoffensive and even insignificant creature should have been so crucially important to all our lives, but what is even more peculiar is the fact that historians across the years have singularly failed to recognise what was right in front of their eyes. Everything we are, all that we have become in our modern, technological world and the whole of Western society stands fairly and squarely on the woolly backs of the ancestors of a billion domestic sheep that inhabit the planet today. The human-sheep association is without doubt the most important symbiotic relationship that humanity has ever experienced and yet the whole story has remained largely unknown.

For me it all started a long time ago. It is many years since I sat in a baking hot goldfish bowl of a classroom and looked out from the third floor of the building across the playing fields towards a low, flat hill in the distance, an area called Abbey Grange. The name of my school was Moor Grange and it was located on the side of a valley scoured out during the last Ice Age. The river is called the Aire and where I grew up the Aire flows through the large and prosperous city of Leeds, in the north east of England.

Like most children I didn't take too much notice of what my teachers were trying to cram into my reluctant head but I did at least have a burning interest in history. I well remember being told for the first time that the local names in this particular part of Leeds were legacies of a building some three or four miles away – a now ruined Cistercian monastery known as Kirkstall Abbey. The word 'Grange', as in Abbey Grange, Moor Grange and Allerton Grange, refers to farms once owned by the abbey. The ruin of Kirkstall Abbey itself is now nothing more than an interesting place to visit on a sunny Sunday but the power and influence it maintained five hundred years ago is still encapsulated in these widespread placenames. Even as an eleven-year-old, it occurred to me just how big the abbey's holdings were and that they must have extended to thousands of acres.

As the years passed I gradually learned more about the remarkable Cistercians – the White Monks who had built Kirkstall Abbey – and I began to realise what a truly significant part they and their large scale sheep rearing had played in the making of the landscape of many parts of Western Europe, and especially that of Great Britain. Eventually, I became a professional writer, with a particular penchant for history from all periods. I read voraciously and learned the art of patient research, which involves not simply looking at a particular historical event, but teasing out the reasons why it happened.

In a distant siding in a remote directory of my successive computers I kept notes on subjects related to research I was undertaking at any given moment but which did not rightfully belong in any specific book. Gradually, the reservoir of facts and information thickened and grew until the various notes began to crystallise into a story about the past and the way it contributed to the present. What resulted at the end of nearly thirty years was at the same time slightly absurd but also extremely compelling. There was absolutely no doubt about it – there was hardly a pivotal event on the long road between our remote past as hunter-gatherers and our ability to land men on the moon that had not been directly responsive to the existence and exploitation of sheep!

"OK", said Chris Knight, a much-respected friend, associate and writing colleague. "So sheep have been significant in historical terms, but then surely so have cattle and pigs!" Had I deluded myself for some reason? I took the time to look again, this time much more carefully, and as a result I was able to convince Chris that I had indeed stumbled across something of great importance – something that historians had completely failed to see.

I cannot deny that sheep have now become something of an obsession for me. Fortunately, it's a gentle madness inspired by the endearing creatures I see on a daily basis, patiently working their way across the rolling acres of the Yorkshire Wolds close to my home.

The one overriding fact that has come from these many years of historical research is this: Humanity has never been involved in a relationship with any other creature that was more pivotal to its development and ultimate success than the one it shares with sheep. I hope that as a result of what follows in this book you, like me, will never look at them in quite the same way again.

A place more fitted for wild beasts...

L ate in May 1152 twenty two tired man arrived at a lonely spot beside the River Aire in West Yorkshire, England. They had travelled for two days from Barnoldswick, an equally wild place on the Pennines, close to Colne. Their point of arrival was little more than a scrubby clearing in the dense thicket but it did already have a name. It was called Kirkstall, probably because there was a tradition of Christian hermits living in the vicinity. The intention of the newcomers was to build an abbey in this desolate setting, on land granted to them by a vassal of Henry De Lacy, a rich benefactor and a powerful nobleman. They had previously settled for a year or two further west, at Barnoldswick, but a combination of terrible weather and hostile locals had forced the relocation.

These were no ordinary monks. They were part of God's new army, zealots to a man and fired with the Holy Spirit in a way that would seem unnatural to the 21st-century mind. They were members of a religious order that was spreading exponentially across Europe and especially within the British Isles. These 'Cistercians' as they had come to be called, owed a duty to the overall mother house of the order, far away at Citeaux in Northern Burgundy and to their founding house of Fountains in North Yorkshire.

Kirkstall Abbey still exists, or at least the majestic ruins of its once grand buildings are still to be seen. It is just a few miles to the north west of the modern city of Leeds. The grounds in which the remains of the abbey stand are now a park, administered by Leeds

City Council. Its custodians are doing all they can to secure what remains of Kirkstall Abbey for the future because despite its roofless state and broken tower it is recognised as being one of the best preserved Cistercian ruins in Britain.

History is composed of millions of events, taking place in thousands of locations across the planet; a spider's web of consequences that in an apparently haphazard way create what we recognise as the present. The focus of humanity is drawn to a specific happening for a brief moment and then attention passes somewhere else. Nevertheless, there are just a handful of places and events that have been so very important that the ripples they make in the water of time never really subside. Kirkstall Abbey is such a location, which seems absurd when one realises that it is barely known outside its own region and also considering the fact that the first Cistercian monks who arrived there had done so almost by chance.

The Cistercians were first and foremost farmers. As an offshoot of the Benedictine order, they recognised the value of hard, physical work, as well as that of incessant prayer. The whole *raison d'etre* of the order was to seek out spots as far from civilization as it could manage, to acquire as much land as possible within a reasonable distance and to create yet another island of self sufficiency in the harsh feudal landscape. When an abbey gained enough land and began to prosper, a group of monks would be sent forth to found another abbey elsewhere. So it had been for five decades when Abbot Alexander and his monks arrived at Kirkstall.

The pattern was always the same. Firstly a church had to be built, together with accommodation for the brothers. Immediately this was done, land would be tilled for vegetable gardens because food was as necessary as prayer. The next job was to clear larger stretches of land and then to enclose them. These would become the 'granges' of the abbey and would be where the cattle, but more especially the sheep, would be put to pasture. Some of the granges could be a day or two's walk from the abbey and they were staffed not by the Choir monks, who were ordained priests, but rather by a new and quite different form of monk. The Cistercians had hit upon the idea of forming a second tier of monks, drawn from the lower echelons of society. These were the lay brothers. Although they took vows of poverty, chastity and obedience, they were not ordained priests but rather 'holy drones' and their presence in the Order had proved inspirational.

Cistercians might have chosen a religious life but they certainly did not retreat from reality in a material sense. They were amongst the best opportunists of their age, exploiting any situation and filling every possible niche in order to better their abbeys and spread more quickly. In England that meant sheep rearing and they made themselves the best and shrewdest sheep farmers Europe had known for at least 3,000 years.

As an example, although Kirkstall was far from being the biggest or most prosperous of the Cistercian houses of England, it would eventually run herds of more than 50,000 sheep. When one bears in mind that there were eventually sixty-eight Cistercian houses in Britain and that Fountains Abbey, the most prosperous of them all, possessed 100,000 sheep[1], the true scale of the operation becomes apparent. It would not be stretching credibility to suggest that the Cistercians in Britain as a whole were running over 1,000,000 sheep. And although they were the most successful sheep farmers of their day there must have been two or three times as many sheep in secular hands. Considering that the population of England at the time of the Doomsday survey in 1087 was no more than two million[2], the true significance of the sheep in the British Isles during this period is obvious.

Cistercian sheep were not bred to feed the rapacious appetites of the monks, who in any case were vegetarians. Only a tiny proportion of the sheep in Cistercian hands would be slaughtered within the abbeys, and these mainly to supply sheepskin for velum, upon which those employed in the scriptorium would meticulously copy out the gospels and other holy books. Rather the Cistercian flocks were kept

---

1   *The White Monks* Glyn Coppack, Tempus Publishing, Stroud, England, 1998
2   General Introduction to Doomsday Book, Henry Ellis, Clearfield Co, London, 1973

for their annual crop of wool. Not that the Cistercians required more than a tiny proportion of the wool for their own needs. The vast bulk of it was destined for export. It found its way to Flanders and to Northern Italy, where it was skilfully transformed into finished cloth. Neither location could procure sufficient raw wool for its manufacturing needs locally and by the 12th century Britain, and in particular England, was probably supplying 60 – 80% of Europe's raw wool needs.

The Cistercians were shrewd and had obtained from the Pope a dispensation from taxes in any country where they settled. Secular wool exporters in England had to pay an export tax when their produce left the country and this went straight into the coffers of the King. Although the Cistercians fed and clothed the brothers of their order; ministered to them when they were ill and looked after them in their dotage, there was no wage bill at the end of each month. With the price of wool remaining high at the time, it is no wonder these abbeys flourished and grew so quickly.

Nobody denies that sheep represented the mainstay of Cistercian life in Britain and everything else that happened within the order was subservient to it. Nevertheless, the 'White Monks' as they were also called, did not rest on their laurels. Every Cistercian house had its own blacksmiths and foundries, and many of them specialised in occupations and crafts aside from sheep rearing, often according to their locations. Some abbeys dug for coal, which was itself quite revolutionary at the time, whilst others excavated iron or lead ore. A particular abbey might specialise in making carts, whilst others bred horses or made farming tools. In this way the Cistercian abbeys helped each other and also produced even more products to sell into society.

For a group of people who were dedicated to isolation and prayer, the Cistercians were surprisingly modern in their outlook and methods. Their tendrils reached out across most of Europe and even beyond to the Near and Middle East. They were quick to pick up on technical innovations and to spread these throughout the family of abbeys. Very recently archaeologists digging on land once owned by Fountains Abbey uncovered what they are sure represents a rudimentary blast furnace. This was a device used to produce good quality iron in quantity and as far as had been previously known it was not invented until the beginning of the 18th century. The example at Fountains dates from the 15th century![3]

The Cistercians were quick to harness waterpower and were accomplished builders and glaziers. They pioneered sewage systems and learned all that was to be known about medicine, both for themselves and their stock. In addition to creating abbeys that were paragons of efficiency and cleanliness, they constructed roads to their more distant granges and streamlined industrial processes in a way that society as a whole would not manage for centuries to come. It has been suggested by many eminent historians that if the Reformation had not spelled the end of the English abbeys in the 16th century, monasticism alone and especially the Cistercians, may have forced the Industrial Revolution to take place in Britain long before it eventually did.[4]

In the organisation of their houses and their very lives the Cistercians offered society a model of democracy that was generally unknown in the feudal states of Europe. The brothers of each abbey met daily in Chapter. There they took all the decisions necessary to the daily running of their abbey and they were responsible for electing its officers – even deciding who should become the Abbot if a vacancy became available. The chosen Abbot of each house travelled each year to the mother house of his own abbey and also to Citeaux, where decisions relating to the entire order were decided by equally democratic means.

Kirkstall Abbey was just one member of a community that eventually numbered well over three hundred abbeys in Europe alone. In its layout, organisation, achievements and ultimate success it was no different than most of its sister abbeys. The factor that sets Kirkstall apart is not so much what it represented, but where it stood. The geographical setting of Kirkstall was due entirely to

---

3   Co-operation of Bradford University and English Heritage, Article *Daily Telegraph*, June 2002

4   Article in *Daily Telegraph*, David Derbyshire, June 2002

prevailing circumstances but these proved to be fortuitous, not so much for the Cistercians, but for the world we live in today. The story of how and why this is the case forms part of the fascinating tale that follows and it has as much to do with geology as it does with any other factor. The tributaries of the River Aire that supplied Kirkstall's needs rise high inland and the river runs between gritstone deposits throughout the whole of its length. Many of the other rivers in Yorkshire originate in and flow through limestone. This fact would be of supreme importance with the passing of time.

There are no sheep at Kirkstall now because the immediate abbey grounds are surrounded by modern developments. The abbey lands of Kirkstall are today filled with houses, schools, factories and offices. Where people now live and work amidst the hustle and bustle of city life, thousands of sheep once grazed peacefully, their yearly crop of wool gradually contributing to our modern world in ways that historians have failed to realise and much of what eventually followed we owe directly to monks like those who arrived at Kirkstall in 1152. Nevertheless, no matter how efficient and forward-looking the Cistercian monks may have been, they certainly didn't 'invent' sheep-rearing – they merely saw a niche and filled it. On the contrary, the domestic sheep had existed in Europe for at least six thousand years and had already proved to be one of the best companions humanity would ever have.

The arrival of the sheep

No animal is more deeply embedded in the psyche of humanity than sheep. Our language is replete with phrases, sayings and idioms related to this animal. We speak about a 'dyed in the wool' individual for someone whose beliefs are particularly deep-seated, but we accuse those who have no specific opinion and who allow themselves to be led around of being 'sheep'. Someone who has been duped and who loses his or her money as a result is said to have been 'fleeced' and if we suspect we are being lied to we might say that a particular individual is 'spinning a yarn'.

If we are forced to take a risk, we may decide to go that extra step because, as we say, 'we might as well be hung for a sheep as a lamb', whilst a woman who tries to convince the world she is much younger or more attractive than she actually is can be unkindly referred to as 'mutton dressed as lamb.' When we cannot follow someone's reasoning we have 'lost the thread' and if we find a person to be particularly annoying we might suggest that, like sheep worried by a dog, they are 'driving us mad'.

It is no wonder at all that sheep figure so prominently in our speech because they represent a primary reason for everything we are – all that we have become across thousands of years of civilization – even if we do not consciously appreciate the fact. Although most of us these days are completely isolated from farming and the land, it isn't so long since our dependence on the countryside was everything to us. Originally the ancestors of everyone reading this book were farmers. The natural response to the flow of the seasons; the needs of planting, harvesting and animal husbandry lie so deep within us that they are endemic. Practically everyone feels less stressed and more at ease when they are amidst the rolling acres or wide fertile plains that once ruled our lives. Sheep were a crucially important part of the farming scene and they were the world's first domestic animal.

There are well over 260 recognised breeds of sheep in the world today but it is certain that all of them ultimately came from just two wild ancestors. The known parent of all modern sheep is the Asiatic Mouflon (*Ovis Orientalis*). This animal, though definitely a sheep, looks very much like a wild goat. It still survives in large numbers in the wild in the mountains of Asia Minor and in Southern Iran and was probably even more widespread before the advent of farming. The Asiatic Mouflon is not a particularly large animal and it appears in a variety of colours, with red predominating. It is closely related to the European Mouflon (*Ovis Orientalis Musimon*), which inhabits Sardinia and Corsica, but it is now thought that the European Mouflon never developed as an independent species and merely represents an example of early, domesticated sheep that escaped and reverted to a wild state.

DNA analysis shows that all modern domestic sheep also have another important ancestor but this seems to have disappeared altogether from the wild. The genes of this mysterious missing parent now survive only in the genes of a billion domestic sheep spread across the planet.

Exactly when the paths of humans and sheep first crossed will never be known for certain. There is no doubt that to our hunter-gatherer ancestors the sheep would have been a significant prey species and it may well have been our preference for mutton that aided our long journey towards farming and a settled life. Over 8,000 years ago it is likely that a hunter somewhere in West Asia killed a wild Mouflon ewe and discovered that she had with her a well-grown lamb. What probably happened is that the hunter had one of those leaps of logic that have set our own species apart. It occurred to him that if he took the lamb back to his nomadic camp and there kept it tethered, it would graze and eventually become a much bigger sheep. It would then be available to eat at a time when hunting wasn't so good and with no effort on his part. Within this idea lay the seeds of animal husbandry and all that followed.

Sheep would have fitted very well with the life of hunter-gatherers who of necessity, were always on the move. The natural tendency of sheep to stay together in flocks allied to the very early domestication of the dog meant that the developing herds could accompany the hunter-gatherers to their seasonal hunting grounds. Thus the first pastoralists appeared and over time the sheep became so important that its needs took precedence over those of the far less reliable hunt. Sheep offered not only meat but also milk, in addition to skins for fine leather and wool for clothing. The wandering continued, but now it was to find the best pasture. There are still many examples of pastoralists to be found in the world and the civilizations that sprang up in the Near and Middle East were founded by such peoples who eventually gave up their nomadic lifestyles. With a settled life, the planting and harvesting of crops also began to take place but this may never have happened, or been considerably delayed, if sheep had not offered such a significant incentive.

As useful as the first domesticated Mouflons might have been, they certainly did not offer the benefits afforded by modern breeds of sheep. The Mouflon had hair rather than wool. Although its skin was probably prized for clothing, it could not be shorn and was almost certainly kept primarily for its meat, though it is possible that milking of sheep was taking place in this remote period. It did not take too long before this situation changed. An archaeological site in Iran revealed a small statue of a sheep that comes from a layer dating back 6,000 years. This statue clearly shows a wool-bearing sheep. This must mean that during a period of 2,000 years a process of selective breeding had been taking place. Shearing was still unknown at this time but wool could be plucked from the animal or collected at the time of the annual moult. Across the two-millennium gap, selective breeding had begun to produce sheep with a greater amount of the woolly undercoat that lay beneath its courser top hair.

From around 5,000 years ago we find many examples of artistic depictions of sheep from the Sumerian culture. These demonstrate many of the characteristics that would be recognised by stockbreeders today.

By 4,500 BC farming had spread west across Europe and both crop planting and animal husbandry had arrived in Britain and other far-flung outposts in the north and west of Europe. It was around this time that the sheep also began to appear, having been brought over from the Continent along with cattle. With Britain's harsh winter climate the first farmers would soon have realised the value of sheepskin for clothes and bed coverings, whilst the living creature could provide milk when other sources of protein were scarce. The meat of the animal would also have been a welcome addition to the diet because protein can be hard to come by and is needed to give strength to survive in an uncertain and cold climate. It is not an exaggeration to say that the presence of the sheep helped a settled existence to take place much further north and west within Europe than would otherwise have been the case.

The sheep immediately had a value that other domestic animals did not. It was a very hardy creature and was not at all fussy about its food. The Mouflon is an animal of the heights. It is a good climber and can search out grazing in areas where other animals would starve. Like their ancestors, the first domesticated sheep were adaptable and tough and as with their wild counterparts they were happy in the uplands, surviving on grazing that was not available to other, less hardy domestic animals. Another great benefit of the sheep was that unlike most of the cattle owned by these early farmers, sheep did not have to be slaughtered ahead of the winter. They could forage in the coldest weather and would be expected to be producing lambs in the early spring, when other food sources were at a premium. Keeping cattle alive in winter was a nightmare until comparatively recent times because it necessitated laying in large amounts of fodder. As a result most cows were dispatched as the winter approached.

The change from a hunter-gatherer existence to that of the settled farmer seems to have been quite rapid, especially in Britain. Michael Richards, an archaeologist at the University of Bradford, England, together with colleagues, analysed the food intake of people living during the Neolithic period in Britain. It seems that around 4,000 BC there was a dramatic and quite sudden change in the diet of those living in the British Isles. Samples of food from pottery shards and an analysis of human bones together confirmed that the habit of eating large quantities of fish and other marine life, which had been the norm during the Mesolithic period (9,000 to 5,200 years ago) [5]stopped quite suddenly, in favour of the flesh of domestic animals. Other ancient sites demonstrate that by far the largest proportion of the meat consumed was mutton. Archaeology in Great Britain also shows that although many sheep were being slaughtered for their meat at around two years of age, many more were much older, a sure indication that wool was being considered an annual crop and had become part of the mainstay of the farming economy.

There were obvious advantages to farming. It wasn't as hit and miss as hunting and it avoided the need to move regularly from one place to another. As a result, populations began to increase rapidly and the almost constant availability of food allowed for a higher degree of specialisation within communities. It also made time available for domestic pursuits, such as spinning and weaving.

Weaving was certainly not something specific to those who first domesticated and altered sheep to have finer coats. On the contrary, an impression of woven cloth of a sort has been found in Pavlov, Morovia that dates back to the Palaeolithic period. This 'ghost' of a fabric, captured in the baked clay of a pot, was produced by a culture known as the Gravettians who flourished as much as 25,000 years ago. Neolithic examples of weaving have also been found in Switzerland, which were most probably made from tree bast or linen. Only with the Bronze Age and the domestication of the sheep did the spinning and weaving of wool take place but the technique was anything but new to the individuals who undertook it. What was new was the quality of the cloth produced and its incredible warmth.

The unique properties of wool originate in its composition. Wool is composed of three layers. The outermost layer of wool is called the

---

5   John Roach, Article, *National Geographic*, "Why did Britons Stop Eating Fish?" Sept 2003

'cuticula'. This is composed of plate-like structures that are protected from the weather by an oily substance known as lanolin. The plates of the cuticula are held together by a glue composed of proteins. Inside the cuticula the wool is divided into two halves that are called the paracortex and the ortocortex. The growth of wool is not symmetrical because the paracortex hardens before the ortocortex. This is what gives wool its 'crimp' or curl, which increases when the wool becomes wet.

A chemical analysis of wool reveals that it is composed of around a hundred proteins that differ from each other in their molecular structure. There are also twenty-two different amino acids in wool, all of which have unique characteristics. Some parts of wool absorb water more than others, which have a tendency to repel it. Even the chemical composition of different elements of the wool varies, with sulphur, acid and alkali predominating in different cases.

Wool is tremendously elastic, which means it retains its shape across time, even when it has been removed from its original owner. Its capacity to absorb water and yet remain effective as an insulator from the cold is little short of incredible. What makes it really special is the fact that when wool gets wet, it releases chemicals that actually make the wearer feel warmer. Woven wool, like its raw counterpart, also produces thermal warmth because of pockets of air trapped between the fibres. When wet, the crimp in wool increases, making its thermal properties even better. In addition, and despite its ability to create warmth when wet, wool is a good water repellent. The surface layers of wool contain tiny pores which allow air to pass through, but which will not admit water. Because of its unique qualities wool allows its wearer, sheep or human, to remain cool when the outside temperature is warm but hotter when the elements are less benign. For all these reasons wool is recognised as being probably the most useful fibre that has ever been made into clothing, either from an animal or a vegetable origin. [6]

Before wool can be woven, it must first be spun, a process that takes the woolly fleece and transforms it into a long, useable thread

---

6   Information gleaned from various publications by Woolmark, Australian Wool Services Ltd

known as yarn. The easiest way of spinning wool is to use a device known as a drop spindle. There is no way of knowing how ancient this device actually is but it is almost certain that it was the way the first farmers prepared the fleece of the sheep for weaving into cloth.

A simple drop spindle
for spinning yarn

Although the simplest machine imaginable, use of the drop spindle is fiendishly awkward until it is eventually mastered. It relies on setting the spindle in motion with one hand, whilst teasing the fleece into a thread with the other. The finished thread is eventually wound onto the spindle and more fleece is added. It is a laborious business but one that must have been used for many thousands of years until the spinning wheel was finally invented in the medieval period.

The thread now had to be woven into cloth. We know that the process of weaving was no mystery and used extensively, because people were already creating fences using materials such as withies. They were also making baskets and elaborate fish traps. Weaving cloth employs the same process.

A woven fence made
from willow

Finger weaving of the type still produced by some Native American peoples probably came first but this cannot produce cloth of a significant width. Undoubtedly the first real looms were extremely simple affairs. A suitable tree was found with a branch that ran close to and parallel with the ground. A series of pieces of yarn were tied to the branch at close intervals and each was weighted with a stone so that it hung down towards the ground. These threads are called the warp. Another thread was now woven in and out of the warp, just as in the case of the willow fence. This second thread is known as the weft. All cloth is produced in this basic manner, even though the mechanisms employed became much more sophisticated with the passing of time. Woollen cloth made in this fairly primitive way would have had a very loose weave but it wouldn't have been long before frames were made that would have kept the threads tighter and which allowed the weft to be pushed up and compacted.

Despite the long passage of time and the improvements in animal breeding, some sheep that would have been common during the Bronze Age in Europe do still exist. It is not surprising that these have survived in the most western and northern fringes of Europe because technological innovations and stock improvements were late arriving in these remote spots. Probably the best example is that of the Soay sheep. The Soay is a small-framed animal with sturdy legs. It varies in colour from light to dark brown and readily sheds its wool in the summer. Male Soay sheep are horned, as are some of the females. Although an extremely primitive example of a domestic sheep, the Soay has a very fine coat, which differs markedly from the Mouflon. In the case of the Soay it is almost impossible to differentiate between the hairy outer and soft inner coats.

Nobody knows how these sheep came to inhabit the Island of Soay, which lies off the west coast of Scotland, but they have certainly been there a very long time. Archaeological evidence tends to support the theory that they were brought to the Island at least 4,000 years ago by Bronze Age settlers. The name of the Island 'Soay' is derived from two Viking words that actually mean 'sheep island' but the animals had been in residence for nearly 3,000 years before the Norsemen arrived.

DNA evidence adds to the logical assumption that the Soay does indeed represent one of the very first efforts to breed a sheep that carries a set of required characteristics. The Soay was a sort of 'utility' sheep because it was and still is used for both wool and mutton. Archaeologists accept that virtually identical animals, though with better flocking instincts than the Island Soay now possesses, once existed across most of Europe and certainly in Britain.

Far from being simply a living fossil, the Soay is once again popular across several continents and particularly so in North America. It represents the ideal 'back-yard' sheep. It is not susceptible to infections and is tougher than most modern breeds. The Soay has also been bred with other sheep to improve specific characteristics and to add strength and endurance, acquired over countless centuries of hard Island life. Soays have small hooves and so don't cause too much land damage in areas where they are put to graze. They can survive on the toughest vegetations and a related breed, in Orkney, has for countless centuries lived on a diet composed predominantly of seaweed.

Soay sheep; probably the oldest surviving wool-bearing breed in the world

Jacob sheep

Obviously sheep bred in other parts of the world during the period of the European Bronze Age had slightly different characteristics, but it seems likely that something very like the Soay once existed from the far reaches of Asia, right across to the extreme western extension of Europe.

Another and perhaps equally ancient breed of sheep is the Jacob. This sheep is altogether more goatlike than the Soay. Jacobs may well have been important to early farmers in and around the Middle East because very similar sheep are shown on Egyptian wall paintings from 1800 BC and on a Sythian gold necklace from at least 1000 BC.

DNA and other evidence points to an Eastern Mediterranean origin for the Jacob. Such sheep also found their way east along the Silk Road to China. The name of the Jacob comes from a book written in the early part of the 20th century by an Englishwoman called Mrs Maude. It concerned sheep that had been bought and sold by her father. She named these sheep and her book 'Jacob's Flock' because very similar animals are mentioned in the Old Testament of the Bible[7]. The Book of Genesis describes how the patriarch Jacob selected and bred spotted sheep as his salary for working in Syria.

Mrs Maude assumed that Jacob had taken his flocks to Egypt, where his son Joseph was employed by the Pharaoh. From there she believed they had been taken into North Africa and thence to Spain, from where they finally found their way up to Britain. Whether or not the story is true, research shows that Jacobs did indeed take this route. They remained quite popular in England before and throughout the middle ages but by the Victorian era they were superseded by more productive species. Jacobs survived as an ornamental species in private parks, mainly because of their good looks and benign temperaments. Like the Soay sheep Jacobs are now bred in large numbers in the US.

Hand spinners in particular love the fleece of the Jacob sheep. The annual fleece weighs an average 3 to 6 pounds and has a long staple (the length of the fibres) of 4 to 7 inches. Jacob wool is soft, with a good lustre but there is not much lanolin (grease) as is the case with some other breeds. The Jacob is another all-round sheep because it is bred as much for meat as for wool.

Another of the really ancient breeds that helped to form later British stocks is the Shetland sheep[8]. As its name implies it was best known from the far Northern Islands of Scotland and was carried back and forth by Scandinavian peoples, being readily bred

---

7   *A History of Jacob Sheep*, Amarinta Aldington, Geering, Ashford, England, 1989
8   *The Encyclopedia of Historic and Endangered Livestock and Poultry Breeds*, Janet Vorwald Dohner, Yale University Press, 2002

in Norway, Sweden and Denmark. A fact that sets the Shetland sheep apart, and which fits it for a hard northern life, is that it can survive well on hay in winter. In this respect it is different to all other breeds, though like most sheep it is also a natural forager, is hardy and needs little veterinarian attention. The Shetland sheep is small in stature and has fine bones and a wedge-shaped tail.

Many Shetland sheep have a 'double fleece'. Whilst the undercoat is extremely fine and is ideal for christening shawls and baby clothes, the outer fleece is coarser with a much longer staple that makes it good for hard-wearing jumpers of the sort that are still worn by fishermen. The meat of the Shetland is low in lipids and is therefore suitable for people who have to watch their cholesterol. Shetland sheep are also now extremely popular on both sides of the Atlantic, despite the fact that this breed fell out of favour for a long period.

Typical Shetland sheep

Sheep are now found in almost all parts of the world, from extremely cold northern regions to the parched sands of the semi desert. They represent one of the most versatile of mammals and can tolerate conditions that other domestic animals would find impossible to endure. Probably the most important realisation and what really sets sheep apart is the fact that no 'major' civilization in the world has ever emerged without them, or at the very least a substitute animal such as the llama that served the same function. There are several reasons for this. First of course comes the value of the sheep as a domestic animal. The sheep has provided wool for clothing, skins for cover and clothing, milk and meat for consumption and valuable manure to enrich poor soils. However, it is my contention that another factor of importance was the value of wool as a 'trade item'.

This made the sheep essential to a way of living that superseded village life when true civilizations began to emerge.

In the cradle of civilization

By around 3,000 BC humanity's long climb towards the world we know today was already underway. At this period farming was already taking place, particularly in that region of the Middle East known as the 'Fertile Crescent'. This is a large swathe of land between the rivers Tigris and Euphrates, much of which now falls within the modern state of Iraq. Prior to 3,000 BC the area had small villages, where planting, harvesting and animal husbandry were already taking place at a subsistence level but the incursion of a fairly mysterious people whose own ancestry still isn't understood altered the situation.

The Sumerians, as the incomers would be known to history, spoke a language quite unlike any other and were not of the same Semitic stock that would eventually predominate across the region. Those arriving at this time had a new and different imperative – something quite unlike anything that had taken place in the world before. They created towns and then small cities, which soon grew and began to control large areas of land. With the passing of time they became the first City States. Within these conurbations all the trappings of civilization originated, giving way to a radically different lifestyle and to technological advances that would push humanity into a different league. Innovations of the Sumerian period include the wheeled vehicle, time and geometrical measurement, a good understanding of astronomy and the invention of writing. [9]

---

9 *Sumer and the Sumerians*, Harriet E W Crawford, Cambridge University Press, 2004

Sumerian cities were usually rectangular in shape and were surrounded by high and wide walls for protection. Within the cities were broad avenues that not only served the daily needs of the population but which were also essential for religious ceremonies. Sumerian religious structures were tall and built in steps. These were known as ziggurats – a sort of artificial mountain upon which temples dedicated to the gods and goddesses of the city were located.

A major feature of every Sumerian city was its markets, where produce from the surrounding area was brought on a regular basis to be bought and sold. Large areas of land in Sumer were given over to agriculture and to the raising of animals. The main crop of the Sumerian period was barley, which in addition to being made into bread was also the chief component in beer, of which the Sumerians were inordinately fond. The growing populations of the cities demanded huge quantities of food, often to be consumed by those who had taken on a high degree of specialisation and who were not food producers themselves.

The Sumerians became great animal breeders and controlled huge herds of sheep. These were not simply a source of protein because their wool clothed practically the entire population. The Sumerians also prized flax, a fibrous plant that is used to create linen, but linen was only worn by the highest echelons of society. To the everyday man and woman of Sumer, wool was essential. By not long after 3,000 BC sheep-rearing represented one of the biggest sectors of the Sumerian economy. Wool allowed warm clothing to be created and this encouraged communities to spread away from the plains around the Tigress and Euphrates and up into the colder mountain regions.

The Sumerians were not alone in their dependence on the sheep around this time. Hot on the heels of the Fertile Crescent, civilization began to develop along the banks of the Nile in Egypt. This area is unique in that it is surrounded on all sides by an arid wasteland but the annual flooding of the Nile offered life-giving silt, brought down by the raging waters from mountains far away. Every year this rich mud would be spread across the margins of the Nile, where it proved invaluable for agriculture and animal husbandry of all kinds. [10]

Like the Sumerians the Egyptians were dependent on the sheep. They used its wool for clothing, its milk as a food and they also prized its meat and skins. Sheep were allowed onto fields that had recently been harvested, as indeed they still are in many parts of the world today. Not only did they eat the remnants of the crop, they also turned over the earth and spread their manure on the land.

Like Sumer, Egypt developed a written language and eventually forged itself into one cohesive kingdom, on the way creating some of the most impressive masterpieces in building that the world has ever known. Both the Sumerians and the Egyptians immortalised the sheep by way of religion. The Sumerians had gods and goddesses whose specific remit was to guard and represent the flocks. The most powerful of these was a Mother goddess by the name of 'Duttur', who was venerated throughout Sumer.

The Egyptians were, if anything, even more in awe of the sheep and the part it played in their society. The very earliest of the Egyptian gods was 'Khnum'. As can be seen in the picture below he had the head of a Ram.

Khnum, the first Egyptian God,
had the head of a Ram

Khnum was worshiped specifically in Egyptian and seems to have been present at the very start of Egyptian civilization. Indeed, some

10 *The Oxford History of Ancient Egypt*, Ian Shaw, Oxford University Press, 2003

of the first inscriptions in Egyptian hieroglyphics make it plain that the worship of Khnum was already ancient before writing was even invented. Khnum was credited with the creation of all the other gods and goddesses of which there were hundreds. To the Egyptians there was no god before Khnum, who was 'self-created'. Khnum made the first egg and from this sprang everything else in creation.

The Ram-headed Khnum was never forgotten by the Egyptians and in fact he seems to have been specifically important to the first Christians, even far from the borders of Egypt itself. His significance doubtless sprang from the importance of the sheep long before Egypt welded itself into a powerful kingdom. The people who came to be the Egyptians had lived in the surrounding areas of North Africa but the climate was changing, making even their pastoral life difficult as the desert closed in. Eventually, they found their way into the Nile Valley and of course they brought their sheep and goats with them. These herds had been important since time out of mind and it is likely that Khnum represented a god whose presence was far older than Egypt itself.

At the same time as the Sumerians and the Egyptians were carving out the rudiments of civilization, other people were abandoning their villages in favour of a city life in Northern India. They are known to us as 'The Indus Valley Civilization'[11] and they occupied territory that lies mainly in modern Pakistan. Also known as the Harappan Culture[12], after the greatest of their cities, these enterprising and intelligent people would eventually build thriving communities based on trade and farming. Unlike the Sumerians and the Egyptians, they were not newcomers and had been in the region since at least 5,000 BC.

Densely packed villages eventually came together to form townships and ultimately fine cities with broad thoroughfares and many civic buildings. The Indus Valley people were great farmers.

---

11   *Ancient Cities of the Indus Valley Civilization,* Johnathon Mark Kenoyer, OUP Pakistan, 1998

12   *Understanding Harappa: Civilization in the Greater Indus Valley,* Shereen Rantagar, Tulika Print Communication Services Pvt Ltd, 2004

They grew barley and wheat and also kept a variety of domestic animals of which sheep seem to have been the most important. Although broadly contemporary with Sumer and Egypt, we know far less about the people of the Indus Valley because although they did possess a written language this has proved impossible to decipher. In addition to wool the Indus Valley Civilization also had another form of textile. They were probably the first people in the world to grow and make use of cotton.

The Indus Valley Civilization mysteriously disappeared between 1800 and 1700 BC. Nobody really knows why, though it is likely that climate change played an important part. Further west, Sumer gave way to the enduring civilization that was Babylonia and the Egyptians remained great for thousands of years and so it was their legacy that passed to the successive cultures of Africa, Asia and Europe.

The sheep had originally been a wild creature of Western Asia but it took quite some time for domestic species to find their way further East. It is thought that sheep only became widespread in China after around 4,000 BC. By this time there were already thriving communities within China, which claims some of the oldest farming in the world. Banpo, a village community near Xi'an, was planting and harvesting rice and other crops between 4,000 and 5,000 BC, and farming was also at an advanced stage along the Yangtze River. Nevertheless, there is no doubt that the introduction of the sheep to China offered a great incentive to emerging civilization in the region as a whole.[13]

However insignificant the sheep may have been to the earliest farmers of China it was destined to take on epic proportions. China now has the largest sheep population of any country in the world at an estimated 130 million. The sheep became so important that the Chinese named one of the zodiac constellations after it. This is the zodiac sign that in the west is known as Cancer the Crab but to the Chinese it is the Sheep or the Ram.

---

13   *China, Its History and Culture,* Scott Morton, McGraw Hill Higher Education, Columbus, Ohio, 2004

With its often-cold climate and despite its own massive herds, the huge population of China has such a need of wool that it now represents Australia's biggest export market for fleeces. Whilst the importance of sheep in the West has diminished somewhat in recent times, the same cannot be said to be the case in China, where the economy remains dependent on sheep and their by-products.

Just as surely as the sheep became enmeshed in the mythologies and religions of the most ancient cultures, so it remains at the core of many modern belief patterns. This is particularly true in the case of two of the world's major religions, Christianity and Islam.

Both Christianity and Islam, together with Judaism, originate from the same historical source. They are responsive to a pastoral people who wandered around the Near East in ancient times and who eventually came to occupy the region that is today known as Palestine. The mythological origin of all these great religions rests on one individual, a man who is mentioned in both the Bible and the Koran. His name was Abraham.

The very first reference to Abraham bears testimony to the importance of the sheep to these nomads, who eventually settled near Hebron, in lower Canaan. The Bible tells us that Abraham worshiped the one true God and that his devotion was so great that he was willing to sacrifice his son on an altar built to the deity. Fortunately for the boy, God intervened and instructed Abraham to sacrifice a ram instead. This particular story had massive implications with the passing of time and ensured that sheep would become an enduring theme in developing belief patterns.

What had been a loose alliance of tribes eventually welded itself into a nation, which became known as the Hebrews. The Bible tells us that a large proportion of the Hebrews eventually became client tribes, living and working amongst the Egyptians in the Nile Delta. Unfortunately for the Hebrews, around 1300 BC Egypt was invaded by the Hyksos, a race that was closely related to the Hebrews themselves. The Hyksos were eventually driven out of Egypt but the Hebrews became very unpopular as a result. Instead of being a client tribe they were now enslaved and would only be rescued thanks to the intervention of one of their most famous leaders, Moses.

Moses may or may not be a real character but the Bible details how, around 1250 BC, he led the Hebrews out of Egypt on an epic journey north that would last 40 years. Eventually they arrived in Palestine, where they fought bitter wars against both the Canaanites and the Philistines, ultimately carving out a kingdom for themselves, with its capital city at Jerusalem. The Hebrews eventually forged the Jewish faith, from which Christianity sprang 2,000 years ago. That part of the Bible that is wholly Judaic in origin is known as the Old Testament, whereas the section that deals with the life of Jesus and what followed is known as the New Testament and is peculiar to Christianity.

In the Old Testament and New Testament combined, the words sheep or lamb occur an amazing 373 times, a testimony to the absolute importance of the creature throughout several thousand years of life in the Near East. Analogies to sheep and lambs are common and particularly so with regard to the sacrificial importance of the animal. This stems in part, not only from Abraham's willingness to sacrifice his own son, and the ram that took the place of the boy, but also because of an incident that is said to have taken place just prior to the Hebrews leaving Egypt.

Moses called down a series of plagues on the Egyptians because they would not let his people leave Egypt. The most horrific of these was the 'killing of the first born', in which the God of the Hebrews visited every house on a single night, killing the oldest son of every Egyptian family. In order to avoid the disaster each Hebrew household had to slaughter a lamb and smear its blood on their doorposts, an echo of the Abraham story. To Jewish people this is known as 'the Passover' and still represents an important annual festival as well as being remembered in regular devotions.

When Christianity arose in the Near East, Jesus, its founder, took on the form of the sacrificial lamb himself. Christians believed that he gave himself up to execution in order to atone for the sins of all his followers. He is often referred to as 'the Lamb of God' but some agencies believe that there are deeper reasons for this state of affairs. Firstly it is possible that aspects of the worship of the Egyptian Ram-headed God Khnum found their way into early

Christianity and the emergence of the Faith also coincided with a significant astronomical period.

Ancient sky-watchers were not aware that the sun lay at the heart of the solar system. Rather they believed that the Earth lay at the centre and that everything revolved around it. Naked eye observations of the heavens revealed a backdrop of stars that remained more or less the same, whilst the sun, moon and planets seemed to travel along a constant path around the sky, which is known as the 'plane of the ecliptic'. Very early in our history the band of stars in front of which the sun, moon and planets pass was split into twelve more or less equal sections, which became known as the signs or constellations of the zodiac. Constellations are groups of stars that although not related seem to form recognisable patterns to which early astronomers gave names. There are twelve zodiac signs and from an Earth-bound perspective it appears that the sun passes from one to another of the zodiac constellations throughout the year, staying a month in each.[14]

In addition to its journey through the zodiac, the sun also appears to rise and set in different places on the horizon throughout each year. At midwinter in the Northern Hemisphere the sun rises south of east, whereas at midsummer it rises north of east. These positions were important to our ancient ancestors because their lives depended upon winter giving way to spring and the abundance of nature returning. The midway point between extreme north and south rising of the sun marked the onset of spring and autumn. These were called the Equinoxes. Traditionally the first day of a New Year was celebrated when the sun was exactly half way on its journey between its rising position in midwinter and that of midsummer, at the Spring Equinox.

One would expect that the part of the zodiac the sun occupied at such times would always remain the same, but this is not the case. The Earth 'wobbles' on its axis like a spinning top across a very long period of time, in fact around 26,000 years for one full revolution. This process is known as the Precession of the Equinoxes. The result

---

14   *The Bronze Age Computer Disc*, Alan Butler, Quantum, Slough, 1997

is that the sun very gradually changes its zodiac position on the important festivals of the year.

At the time of Jesus, around 2,000 years ago, the sun rose on the first day of the New Year (at the Spring Equinox) in the zodiac sign of Aries, which is the sign of the Ram. Because of the peculiarity of the Precession of the Equinoxes, the sun's position at New Year moves not forwards, but backwards through the zodiac. Two thousand years or so before the birth of Jesus, the sun rose at the time of the Spring Equinox in the zodiac sign of Taurus the Bull. This may partly explain why bull worship was so prevalent during that era. In fact the forefathers of the Jewish religion experienced great difficulties in trying to prevent people from openly worshiping bulls, a practice that was also strong in Egypt and which is referred to in the Bible in the Book of Exodus that carries the famous story of the Golden Calf.

Just for the record, although astrologers still say that the sun occupies one degree of the sign of Aries on 21 March each year, this is not actually the case. In reality it presently rises between Pisces and Aquarius on the day of the Spring Equinox because the Earth has wobbled a little more since the time of Jesus.

The Ancient Greeks, who were looking at the stars long before Christianity came along, told their own stories about the zodiac sign of Aries but the association with sacrifice was already in place. To the Greeks this was the story of a beautiful Princess, Andromeda, who was about to be sacrificed to a terrible sea monster known as 'Cetus' but who was rescued by the heroic Perseus.

The constellation of Aries also related specifically to another Greek story, that of Phrixus, the son of King Athamus of Boetia. The King had grown tired of his first wife, Nephele, and had put her aside to marry another woman called Ino. Ino was very jealous of the King's children by his first wife and did her best to kill them. The God Heracles sent a golden ram to save Phrixus, which carried him to far off Colchis where, rather unfortunately, the brave ram was sacrificed. Nevertheless, as a mark of respect to its heroism the ram was translated to the stars by Zeus, king of the Gods. It remains today as the constellation and zodiac sign of Aries.

Another great world religion, Islam, originates from the same rootstock as Judaism and it developed in the same geographical area. Both beliefs consider Abraham to have been their common ancestor. Worshippers of Islam are known as Muslims and they have a particular reverence for a 6th-century prophet by the name of Mohammed. The Holy Book of Islam is called the Koran. Although specific mentions of sheep are not so common in the Koran as they are in the Bible they do exist, and there isn't any doubt about the importance of the sheep to the Muslims, who spread their faith across the whole of Arabia during the 7th century. Muslims represented a broad cross section of pastoralists and farmers but all were very reliant on sheep.

In the following century Muslims from North Africa conquered parts of what is today known as Spain. They settled in the south of the Iberian Peninsula and were not finally evicted until the 15th century. During their stay the area underwent a transformation in farming and culture generally. It was at this time that new breeds of sheep were introduced into Spain, which would ultimately lead to the Merino, the most famous breed of sheep in the world today.

Even by the time the Muslim Moors invaded Spain, the sheep was already spread far and wide across Europe and Asia. New breeds already existed and the importance of the animal was well established almost everywhere. In order to understand how this happened we have to look specifically at two cultures that would have a profound bearing the world we know today. These were the Greeks and the Romans.

The Golden Fleece

The civilization we refer to as Classical Greece dates from around 500 BC and this culture was vitally important to everything that came later. The region now known as Greece had been inhabited and in some cases already civilized long before the Classical period. Ancient Greece received its incentive for organised life and for its eventual ideals from a number of different sources. However, no culture ultimately gave more to that of Classical Greece than a civilization that flourished on the nearby Island of Crete and which reached its zenith as early as 2,000 BC.

This was the culture of the Minoans that although often mentioned in ancient documents, never began to fill the pages of known history until the early years of the 20th century. By way of Greece and its colonies and trading ports elsewhere, no civilization ultimately offered more to European culture than that of the Minoans who represented Europe's first super civilization[15]. A particularly important factor is that through the Minoans we have some very accurate records of what was happening in Crete, a unique state of affairs at such an early period in Europe.

It was in the early years of the 20th century that a rich aristocrat from England first turned his attention towards Crete. His name was Sir Arthur Evans and he was a gentleman archaeologist. Evans had heard of a great mound, not far from Herakleon the modern

---

15 *The Bronze Age Computer Disc*, Alan Butler, Quantum, Slough, 1997

capital of Crete. Some people believed that beneath the mound lay the fabled Labyrinth of mythology, where Theseus was said to have battled with the half-man, half-bull Minotaur, aided by the beautiful Ariadne. She provided Theseus with a spool of woollen thread so that he could find his way back through the Labyrinth.

Evans bought the land in question and it didn't take him long to discover what lay beneath. Archaeology was rocked in the 1920s by the discovery of the tomb of Tutankhamun in Egypt but in reality Arthur Evan's patient work across decades on the ruins of the palace of Knossos in Crete contributed much more to our understanding of ancient history. Evans did not know what the builders of Knossos had called themselves. He christened them the Minoans after Minos, the legendary King of Crete, and the unearthing of this civilization brought to light a society that was far more fabulous than even the richest legends suggested.

The lifetime's work of Evans, together with the hundreds of archaeologists since who have dug sites in other parts of Crete has gradually built a picture of what amounts to an island paradise. By around 2,000 BC Crete was dominated by four large palaces, which in addition to being religious and ceremonial centres, also represented the economic hub of Minoan society. The largest of these was Knossos, an amazing complex built across dozens of acres and containing literally hundreds of rooms. At a time when most of the inhabitants of Europe were still living in crude huts, Knossos had sophisticated drainage, ingenious light wells, fabulous gardens and even flushing toilets.

Crete is a large island with significant farmland and many natural treasures, but it could never have grown to such power in the European Bronze Age if its people had stayed within their own Mediterranean fastness. The Minoan civilization relied absolutely on its ability to trade and as a result developed a great merchant and fighting fleet that sailed the length and breadth of the Mediterranean, all around the Aegean Sea and up into the Black Sea area. Minoan traders almost certainly passed through the Pillars of Hercules and out into the Atlantic Ocean and they may well have extended their trading ties as far as Britain.

What the Minoans needed most was something their island lacked – the means to create bronze. For this they required both copper and tin and they went a long way to find it. In return they offered honey, olive oil, wonderful delicate pottery that was centuries ahead of anything else available, golden objects of great beauty and probably most important of all, wool in abundance.

Minoan Crete developed not one but two forms of writing. The first, which can be seen on a remarkable little clay disc found in the palace of Phaistos, was composed of hieroglyphs, not unlike those used in Egypt, but there was also a later script which was not hieroglyphic in nature and which had become known as Linear A. Unfortunately, mainly because we have no idea of the language spoken in Minoan Crete, Linear A cannot be deciphered. More fortunately for us, if not for the Minoans themselves, a natural disaster that took place around 1500 BC, meant a change of government in Crete and the adoption of a new script we can understand.

Probably around 1450 BC the volcanic island of Santorini, also known as Thera, exploded with a ferocity never previously experienced by humanity. It devastated the entire region and because it was so close to Crete it also seems to have destroyed a large section of the infrastructure of the Island. For reasons that are not altogether understood this allowed the Minoans to fall under the domination of another culture, known as the Mycenaeans, which was beginning to gain ground on the mainland of Greece. Though clearly damaged by the eruption of Santorini, Crete continued to be rich in its resources, which were carefully catalogued by the new Mycenaean overlords. As a result a series of baked clay tablets found in Knossos show just how rich and successful Minoan society was, and from where that wealth came.

The tablets tell us that in the period immediately after the Mycenaeans began to dominate the island, the Palace of Knossos alone was running 100,000 sheep![16] Knossos was one of four known palaces on the island and even if we allow for the fact that it was

---

16 *The Bronze Age Computer Disc*, Alan Butler, Quantum, Slough, 1997

the largest palace, there are other considerations to bear in mind. Evidence shows that a high degree of individual initiative existed within Minoan society. The wealth of the palaces certainly did not represent everything that was happening on the island – far from it. This was a society that exemplified a merchant-led economy. We can be certain that the 100,000 sheep owned by Knossos was only a small proportion of those that existed across the Island and there may have been well over half a million sheep in total or even substantially more.

The population of Crete was not great and the sheep were not being raised in such quantities for home consumption. In any case the Linear B tablets make it plain that the reason for so many sheep was the production of wool, most of which was intended for trade purposes. Some sheep may have been exported live from Crete, maybe to improve breeds elsewhere, but selling mutton would not have been an option bearing in mind the length of the voyages Cretan ships embarked upon. Amongst the symbols that occur time and again in the early Minoan hieroglyphic writing is one that looks strikingly like the fleece of a sheep. It is becoming more and more likely that the exportation of wool was a significant factor in the rise of Minoan Crete and that its other exports, no matter how beautiful, were moderate in comparison.

Other Linear B inscriptions found in Mycenae, which is situated on the Greek mainland, demonstrate that sheep-rearing was also taking place there in the years after 1500 BC, but on a very much smaller scale. Here the numbers mentioned are only 10,000 but it seems that the Mycenaeans were quick to learn from the Minoans because wool also became the mainstay of their own emerging civilization. In later times it can be seen that sheep-breeding both for home needs and with an eye to trade passed to many of the cultures of the Aegean that would add to the rise of Classical Greece.

A story that appeared in the period during which Mycenae was at its most powerful was that of Jason and the Argonauts. This tale is of Bronze Age origin and details the adventures of Jason, the rightful heir of the king of Iolcus. Ioclus lay in a region of Greece where the Mycenaeans predominated. Jason's uncle, Pelias, had usurped the throne whilst Jason was still a child and would have killed Jason except for the fact that his mother had pretended that her son had died in infancy.

The Queen of all the Gods, Hera, hated Pelias because he refused to worship her and so she determined to destroy him. She chose to do so via Jason, who, when he had grown sufficiently, set off to Iolcus to reclaim his rightful throne. King Pelias had different ideas. In order to get rid of Jason he sent him off on an epic quest to find and bring back to Greece the Golden Fleece. This was the fleece of the ram Chrysomallus that had been created by Zeus and which had carried an earlier hero, Phrixus, to Colchis. It is also the ram depicted as the sign of Aries in the zodiac.

Colchis was located at the far end of the Black Sea, which represented an epic voyage in Bronze Age times but Jason set off on a wonderful ship called the *Argo*, with a band of heroic companions who became known as the Argonauts. After many adventures the Golden Fleece was found and Jason returned home with it in triumph.

The story of Jason and the Argonauts is just that – a story, but underpinning it could be an account of the extent of the trading routes used by the Mycenaeans and it might also indicate a less well-known but important use for wool in that remote period. The streams and rivers of Colchis and the region in which it flourished were rich in gold but the metal was not easy to recover because it was in tiny particles. One method, which is still used in some parts of the world today, is to place the fleece of a sheep in the running water of a gold-bearing stream. As if by magic the small particles of gold become trapped in the wool and can be recovered periodically. Unlike panning for gold, which requires constant attention for a very small gain in gold, the same person can service dozens of fleeces and consequently collect far more gold.

This method of obtaining gold may well represent the origin of the Golden Fleece but yet another truth could underpin Jason's epic adventure. It is more than likely that Mycenaeans trading for gold with the inhabitants of Colchis, paid for the precious metal with the commodity that had always been of importance to them, and to their predecessors the Minoans. In other words, gold was traded for wool. The Minoans had been adept at sheep breeding and were doubtless producing wool of a very high quality. This wool would be prized by the inhabitants of Colchis – just as the gold that was common in Colchis was coveted by the Mycenaeans.

Mycenae fell in about 1100 BC, as hoards of newcomers from further north poured down into the body of Greece. This period was a dark age for the region but from it emerged that great flowering of civilization we call Classical Greece.

By 800 BC a number of powerful city-states were beginning to emerge on the Greek mainland. These were ruled by a group of more or less despotic leaders who have become known to history as 'the tyrants'. This was also a time of colonization, during which Greek influence and power was beginning to spread around the Mediterranean and up into the Black Sea.[17]

The various city-states of Greece, although they had fought each other extensively, were forced together by a common danger, that of the Persian Empire. In 493 BC they faced King Darius, who had landed in Greece with a huge army. Darius was defeated by the Greeks, as was Xerxes some years later. It was from this point on that Athens began to assume the role of the most powerful and influential of the city-states and the time when it began to experiment with democracy. Athens and the surrounding states became the home of great ideas, of logic and scientific experimentation. Greece grew rich and powerful from its conquests and imports but in its own domestic arrangements it remained what it had always been, a land of valleys and high mountains.

Greece has never been a geographical location that allowed farming to take place on a great scale. It is, as it has always been, a grower of olives, grapes, citrus fruits and vegetables. It was able to grow enough wheat to supply its populace with bread and being surrounded by the sea Greeks were, and remain, great consumers of fish. Even during its golden age most of those living within Greece survived as they had always done, as small-scale farmers on family

---

17   *The Greeks*, Penguin History, H D F Kitto, Penguin Books, London, 1991

owned plots. Nevertheless, the landscape across much of the area was ideal for the breeding and grazing of both goats and sheep, which together with donkeys were the mainstay of animal husbandry. It is difficult to know whether exports of wool were significant during the Classical Age because there are no records from the period. Whether or not these were taking place, the domestic market for wool was certainly significant.

The climate of Greece tends to be very hot in the summer but somewhat chilly in the winter months. Clothes reflected this fact and certainly up to around the 5th century BC, even affluent people wore clothes made exclusively from wool. We may not know much about Greek exports but we know a great deal about what was worn at the time because the Greeks have left us thousands of beautifully created statues that depict every item of clothing from the era.

The basic costume for women was a garment known as the Doric Peplos. It was made from a rectangle of woven wool, about six feet in width and eighteen inches more in length than the height of the person for whom it was intended. The fabric was wrapped around the wearer in a very simple way, with the excess material folded over the top. It was held in place by pins at both shoulders and the extra material could be wrapped around the head if the weather was really cold. A later costume that became popular for women was the Ionic Chiton. This was similar to the Peplos but was much wider. Having no surplus material it was made specifically for the wearer and was cut to the exact size from shoulder to ankle. Because this garment was up to ten feet in width, it must have been very heavy and its dimensions show clearly that there can have been no shortage of wool. As Greek society became more affluent the woollen Chiton was replaced by one of linen or even silk for the few who could afford such material.

A similar costume was worn by men, though after the 5th century BC the full length Chiton was replaced by one that reached down to the knees. In summer it could be pinned in such a way as to leave one shoulder bared and like the clothes of the women it was almost always made from wool. Until Greece really began to command territories away from its own shores even rich people would have had little choice but to dress in wool and for the vast majority of Greeks, this remained the only fabric available. It is therefore evident that the sheep held an important and lasting role in Greek agriculture.

As early as 1000 BC groups of people who would eventually be Latin speakers began to settle in the area that is now the city of Rome in Italy. There they farmed; they kept pigs, cattle, sheep and goats and lived in fairly primitive dwellings. Rome is close to the sea and those living in this area gradually began to foster trade contacts. They were brought into contact with Greek civilization, from which they learned a great deal and they also drew heavily from the existent culture of the Etruscans, whose domains bordered their own territory.

By 510 BC Rome had undergone a series of changes and was beginning to become a cohesive society. It eventually threw aside its kings and formed a republic. From this point on the Romans began to expand and to gradually overthrow all the other regions of Italy. Rome was a very martial society and its army developed quickly once the conquests began. More and more regions gradually fell to Rome, which became an Empire in its own right. Roman rule eventually stretched across much of Europe, parts of Asia and chunks of Africa. In 57 BC Rome conquered Gaul, now France, and in 43 AD it attacked and subdued large sections of the British Isles.

Whatever the wrongs of Roman rule, it did have a civilizing influence in many of the regions that fell under its sway. Such a large empire allowed new ideas to spread from one region to another and this was as true with animal husbandry as it was in other circumstances. Many new breeds of sheep appeared at this time. One of these still survives and its name bears testimony to its origins. It is called the 'Rufain' sheep and is to be found in Wroxeter in England and also in farms across Wales. The word Rufain is Welsh for Roman. The Rufain is often mistaken for a goat but it is a strong black and white sheep with good characteristics. Another British sheep influenced or perhaps even introduced by the Romans is the Cotswold. This is a large white-faced sheep with an extremely desirable fleece. The area of England known as the Cotswolds did not give its name to the sheep, but rather the other way round. The name Cotswold is a combination of 'Cot' from the cots or enclosures where the sheep were kept and 'wolds', which is a descriptive word for open, hilly ground.

The Cotswold sheep was amongst the first breeds to be taken to the US where it flourished, especially in the south. It forms one of the genetic pools from which many more modern breeds are derived.

The Romans were also responsible for the creation of a direct ancestor of the Merino sheep. It is suggested that an animal of this type first appeared during the reign of the Emperor Claudius, (41–54 AD). The Merino is the best wool-bearing sheep in the world and although it originated in Italy it was then taken to Spain where it prospered and became even more refined. The wool of the Merino represented the backbone of the Spanish economy in early modern times and was instrumental in the creation of a famous French breed known as the Rambouillet. Sheep of a Merino type now predominate in Australia and New Zealand.

Although the Romans were great sheep eaters, they also had to be clothed. The most famous of all Roman garments was the toga. This was a costume that bespoke both power and wealth. The toga was a large rectangle of white woollen cloth, similar to the Greek Chiton. Only in later Roman times was this garment made from linen and even then only for the elite. A more modest and common garment for men was a woollen tunic, topped when necessary with a woollen cloak. Women also wore tunics, over which they usually placed a robe, called a 'stola', which reached down to the ankles. Except for the most prosperous of Romans all these garments were made of wool, another indication that the importance of the sheep remained throughout the whole of Europe and Asia as well is in parts of Africa, throughout the whole span of ancient history.

As far as Britain was concerned, when the Romans retreated at the start of the 5th century, a period of uncertainty, invasion and huge social change began. Filling the void left by the withdrawal of the Legions came waves of warriors from Flanders, Fresia and Germany. These people became collectively known as the Anglo Saxons and this period is known as the Dark Ages, because historical records are almost nonexistent. France had fallen under the influence of tribes from across the Rhine – the very people who would give their name to the country. These people were the Franks and one particular group, the Merovingians, would come to dominate the whole region. Agriculture on both sides of the English Channel doubtless continued in much the way it always had, though there were differences. Both regions had been dominated for centuries by powerful Roman villas, huge farms that became very productive. Outside the lands of the villa life had retained a tribal element with small farmsteads clinging to crude houses in village economies. With the retreat of the Romans both France and England gradually began to take on a feudal economy. The first warlords of the Dark Ages eventually gave way to rulers of regions, who, with the passing of generations, consolidated their holdings and became kings.

The structure of feudal systems was shaped like a pyramid, with the King at the top and several layers of greater and lesser Barons below him. At the bottom were the peasants and the serfs, who had few rights. Everyone in feudal society owed a duty or 'fealty' to those above them and ultimately to the king. The barons supported the king in times of war, drawing men from their own retinues and villages, supported by their manors, where the raw materials of life were created.

Manors were areas of land held by a particular lord. They might contain one or a number of villages and possibly hundreds or thousands of acres of land. Usually a third of the land on each manor was held for the lord and another section was given to the local church. The available land comprised forest, common land, pasture and land for cultivation. Those who worked the land included freemen or peasants, serfs and slaves. The areas set aside for crops was split into strips and then shared out, so that everyone got a fair proportion of both good and bad land. The working week of the peasant was split between his obligations to his lord, to the church and to his own cultivation and he might spend half a week fulfilling his responsibilities to the lord of the manor before getting round to supporting himself and his family.

Peasants had few rights but they were better off than the serfs, who were themselves little better than slaves. The serf was bound to his lord for life and he could never leave the manor unless he was brave enough to run away. If he tried to do so, and was caught, the punishment was severe.

There were differences in the structure of France and Anglo Saxon England, but these were minimal and disappeared altogether after the Norman Conquest of 1066, at which time William, Duke of Normandy, took possession of England. He became king after a great battle in which the Anglo Saxon King, Harold, was killed. We know from the few records that survive that sheep rearing in Anglo Saxon England was already extremely important before 1066, not only in terms of domestic needs but also a means by which trade could be undertaken with other countries. However, the full extent of sheep rearing in England during this period only becomes obvious at the time of the Doomsday Survey. Once England was secure, William wanted to know exactly what he owned in his new kingdom. In 1086 he sent clerks and scribes all over England, to catalogue everything they found, down to the smallest detail. This was the first survey of its kind in England and it reveals one over-riding fact.

Although livestock in England at the time included cattle, pigs, fowl and goats, by far the most predominant species was the sheep. There were in fact far more sheep in England in 1087 than all the other animals put together. It is certain that William was aware of this situation prior to 1066. Attacking England had been a risky venture and one that might easily have failed. William had only been able to undertake the challenge by enlisting the support of lords and knights who came from regions far from his own domains. Both he and they expected a handsome return on their investment and the knowledge of England's huge numbers of sheep would have been a major incentive.

All the same sheep breeding, like everything else in the agricultural economy, was a very local, inefficient and piecemeal business, even after the Normans were running the country. It would take the industry, ingenuity and organisational skills of the Cistercians monks to teach people how sheep rearing ought to be undertaken.

Holy sheep

The Cistercian order had been created in Citeaux, Burgundy, in 1098 as a response to the lax ways and luxurious lifestyles enjoyed by Benedictine Monks at the time. The Benedictines or Black Monks had been in existence since around 600 AD and had many abbeys throughout Europe. The passing of time found them becoming ever more prosperous and it was felt by some within the order itself that their true calling had been forgotten. A number of reformed Benedictine abbeys sprang up in the late 11th and early 12th centuries and the Cistercians represented one of these. [18]

The man who really put the Cistercians on the map is known to us today as St Bernard of Clairvaux. He was born in Northern Burgundy in 1090 and joined the order of the Cistercians in 1113. He had not come alone to Citeaux but had brought up to thirty of his relatives with him and between them they virtually hijacked the new order. Bernard was not just any prospective monk. He was the son of a very influential aristocratic family from Fontainnes de Dijon and he had relatives in high places. Up until the arrival of Bernard, the Cistercians had been struggling even to sustain one small monastery but within a very short time the order was spreading its tendrils far and wide.

---

18 *Cistercians in the Late Middle Ages (Studies in Medieval Cistercian History)*, edited by E Roanne Elder, Cistercian Publications, 1982

It was the influence of Bernard that created the first Cistercian abbeys in England. The abbey that would become the most powerful of them all, Fountains in North Yorkshire, fell under his jurisdiction and protection. Bernard was related to and on very good terms with the Count of Burgundy, a very powerful Baron who also happened to own lands far north of Burgundy itself. In particular the Count had interests in Flanders, which took in parts of modern Northern France, Belgium and Holland. By the early 14th century Burgundy would come to rule Flanders completely. Many Cistercian houses were established in Flanders, where the monks helped in reclaiming vast areas of land from the sea, a process to which monasticism had already contributed since the 9th century. This gave Bernard an even stronger connection with the region. The people of Flanders were enterprising, determined and fiercely independent. As early as the 11th century, those in the region had turned their attention to ways of earning a living other than by farming. In particular they began to excel at spinning, weaving and dying wool.

The only problem they faced was that they could not raise sufficient sheep with good quality wool to keep pace with their needs. Doubtless this fact was one of the subjects that came up in conversations between the Counts of Burgundy and Champagne and their kinsman Bernard. A mutually advantageous solution soon presented itself.

The Cistercians were not merely innovators but also inspirational improvers. For example, the rearing of sheep and the export of wool by monks from England was by no means a new phenomenon when the Cistercians arrived in the 12th century. On the contrary, it had been taking place for some time. As just one example for which we have documented evidence, around 1040 Leofric, a powerful Anglo Saxon Lord, together with his wife Godiva, founded a Benedictine abbey close to Coventry. The monks there became famous for their excellent sheep and in fact the area continued to be significant to the wool trade right up until the 18th century. The Benedictine wool from this abbey and others was almost certainly exported to Flanders, the main area of Europe where the finished cloth trade was already being established. Unfortunately the circumstances under which the Benedictines ran their abbeys meant that theirs would never be more than a small-scale venture in comparison with what was to follow.

With his impeccable connections and rising influence, Bernard of Clairvaux was able to take a number of existing ideas and to squeeze the last drop of profit from them. The very nature of Cistercian monasticism proved to be the important factor. Benedictine monks, having been established for such a long period, 'fitted in' to the medieval landscape. They became lords of manors and administered these much as any other landowner might. This was fine as far as it went but it did not compare with the Cistercian way of doing things. The Cistercians did not need peasants or serfs because they had their own underclass – the lay brothers. They preferred not to become involved with the inefficiencies of the feudal system, but rather to create their own social and economic structure. With the dispensations they had from successive popes they paid no taxes and owed no fealty, no matter where they chose to settle.

Bernard of Clairvaux enjoyed good contacts far from Champagne, where his own abbey was situated, and it was probably he who realised that there was a fortune to be made by anyone who could raise sheep efficiently in Britain and export their wool on a massive scale. This is exactly what happened. Wool from the annual shearing of the sheep on the Cistercian lands was brought back to each abbey from the granges, where it was cleaned and sorted. From there it was taken to a regional collection point. It was then despatched to the nearest port and shipped to Flanders and, to a lesser extent, to Italy. The Cistercians also came to act as intermediaries for other wool producers and what made their enterprise much more successful than that of the earlier Benedictines was the economy of scale involved. As a result the Cistercian abbeys of England became fabulously rich.

The Cistercians also did something else that would have a profound bearing on the development of Great Britain, even after their own demise. Whereas land in England was divided into small strips that were wasteful and inefficient, the Cistercians abandoned the manorial strip system and opened up large areas, which they then enclosed behind fences. In so doing they created pasture for hundreds if not thousands of sheep. Much of the land they used had been marginal and of no real agricultural use but the willing sheep, by foraging on the land and also spreading their manure across it, eventually created first-rate agricultural acres. This process was known as enclosure and it would eventually change the face of the British Isles and destroy social structures that had existed for centuries.

There was one slight fly in the ointment for the Cistercians, which arose from the vows they took as monks. In general, they were not allowed to travel, except to mother houses or to Citeaux. Such a rapidly expanding business empire demanded that the circumstances of transportation in particular became as efficient as that of production, but the Cistercians were hardly in a position to enter the realms of haulage or shipping. This would have become something of a problem had it not been for another brainwave that originated in both Burgundy and Champagne. The result was the creation of an order of fighting monks that became known as the Knights Templar.

The forces of Christianity had attacked the Muslim-dominated Near East during the First Crusade and had conquered Jerusalem in 1099. With the Holy Land and much of the Near East now in Christian hands, the potential for trade was growing rapidly. In 1128 Bernard of Clairvaux established a way through which his own home region could gain from this state of affairs, whilst at the same time answering the Cistercian's problems. For some time, in fact since 1118, a small group of aristocratic knights, mainly from Champagne, Burgundy and Flanders, had been living in accommodation close to the palace of the King of Jerusalem, on the Temple Mound, on the site where the famed Temple of Solomon once stood. They had travelled to Jerusalem with a vow to protect pilgrims travelling the roads from the Mediterranean ports to the Holy City but their real motivation was almost certainly different.

Bernard of Clairvaux had great influence with the popes of his time. He made the suggestion that if this small band of holy warriors, many of whom were his relatives, were formalised as a monastic order representing the nucleus of a great army dedicated to the service of God. The Pope at the time, Honorius II, took the bait. The knights, under the leadership of Hughes de Payen, were recalled to France where they became 'The Poor Knights of Christ and the Temple of Solomon' – better known to us as the Knights Templar.

The rules of this new order were written by Bernard himself and were based on those of the Cistercians. The Templars would become a formidable army, that fought with distinction in the Near and Middle East but they were much more, as had clearly intended to be the case.

Hundreds of knights flocked to the new order. They were most commonly the younger sons of landed lords, whose only other resort was to join the Church as monks or priests. The prospect of fighting the infidel must have seemed preferable to a quiet, cloistered life and at the same time their disappearance from ordinary society had a stabilizing influence because many of them had been hotheaded troublemakers. Grants of money and land also flooded in, giving the Knights Templar the capital they needed to fund their undertakings.

Like the Cistercians the Templars became efficient and productive farmers. They too created profitable farms and mastered the art of rearing sheep in large quantities. This would prove important to the early economy of the order but it represented only a small part of the Templars' ultimate ability for creating wealth.

Almost at its inception the order began to create a formidable array of ships, both fighting craft and merchantmen. This wasn't surprising. How else would it be able to get its troops and other personnel back and forth from the Holy Land? However, the Templars were soon using their fleet in other ways. They began by ferrying pilgrims back and forth across the Mediterranean – at a price, and they were soon also carrying cargoes that had nothing to do with their own needs.

The Knights Templar soon represented a vast moneymaking machine and one that always had an eye on the needs of Burgundy, Champagne and Flanders. As a natural extension of their cargo-handling the Templars also began to act as bankers, both to merchants and to individuals. They created their own ports both on the Continent and in Britain, two examples being Boston in Lincolnshire and Bristol on the west coast in Avon. The Templars not only exported their own wool from these places but also that of their monastic cousins, the Cistercians.

As part of the same cohesive plan the Counts of Champagne, where the Templars had their European headquarters, began to expand their local markets. These eventually grew into huge, international affairs and became famous as the 'Champagne fairs'. Held at various times of the year and in different cities, the Champagne fairs attracted merchants from all around the known world. There, luxury products from the East met woollen cloth that had been brought down from Flanders, on roads that were also often made and patrolled by the Templar order.

The authorities in Champagne and Burgundy were probably not in the least concerned about the well-being of the English economy but as the demand for finished woollen cloth increased, so the producers in Italy, and especially in Flanders, grew busier. This meant they needed more fleeces, which was excellent news for the Cistercians and also for the Knights Templar. Of course it was also useful for the economy of England generally because as big as the Cistercians and Templars were as sheep-breeders, they would always be eclipsed by the great mass of the population, who were also raising sheep. Everyone who was able to do so kept a small flock, or even just one or two animals. Sheep meant an annual cash crop that bolstered any meagre family income. In many parts of the world it still does!

Across the water in Flanders things were going very well by the end of the 12th century. One of the largest areas for processing the English wool was in and around the city of Ghent. The city stood at the confluence of the rivers Scheldt and Leie. It certainly wasn't a new settlement because its credentials as an area of spinning and weaving almost certainly went back to Roman times. In the 7th century Ghent gained an impressive new cathedral and later it gained another. The city was well placed to attract both raw materials and workers from the surrounding areas. It became so important that the Emperor Charlemagne gave it a fleet of ships to protect it from Viking raids, though even then it was sacked twice during the 9th century. Ghent recovered from the setbacks and built itself a fine set of stone walls to keep out future prospective invaders.

As the start of the 13th century Ghent, together with other important cities in Flanders, such as Bruges, Antwerp, St Omar and Lille, was producing some of the finest cloth available in Europe. A great expertise in dying cloth was also developing, with numerous bright colours available. Finished cloth from the Flanders region found its way overland to Italy and the Mediterranean, as well as into the Near and Middle East, most commonly via the Champagne fairs, where credit markets were beginning to take shape. All this success made the citizens of Flanders anxious to retain their monopolies, even within their own territories. There was fierce competition between the largest cities, which sometimes spilled over into open conflict.

In an effort to maintain their hold over the finished cloth market, the producers of Flanders began to band together into organisations known as guilds. Guilds were a cross between a trade federation and the trade unions because they were designed to protect everyone involved in a specific trade, from the lowest to the highest. In reality the ordinary workers had little say in the workings of the guilds and neither did they have any control over the running of the cities and towns in which they laboured. Ever more sophisticated infrastructures led to greater taxes imposed upon the townspeople, which as time went by became a disincentive to cloth production concentrated in areas of urban settlement. This is probably one of the reasons why industrialisation of cloth making and finishing did not take place sooner than it did. It became far cheaper to produce the cloth in rural areas and to take it to the cities for sale and shipment.

Although by far the vast majority of wool was being exported from England in its raw state during the 12th century, there were already places where finished wool production was taking place and had been doing so for quite some time. When William the Conqueror had invaded England in 1066, he had brought a significant number of Flemmings with him – both highborn lords and commoners who fought in his army. Some of them chose to settle in England and other people were encouraged to leave Flanders for a new life on the English side of the Channel. Many of the newcomers were spinners and weavers who settled in and around London, where they produced high quality cloth for export, though as yet England was making little progress in the export of cheaper, thinner cloths for the Mediterranean market.

Paradoxically, the English and in fact the British as a whole, continued to buy most of the cloth they needed from the Continent. This was a rather strange departure for a country whose raw woollen production was outstripping any other region of Europe and is something of a puzzle. Clearly it makes no economic sense whatsoever to raise hundreds of thousands of sheep, to then sell the wool for export, only to have to pay for both production and transportation in order to buy the same wool back as finished cloth.

Part of the reason lay in the nature of English society at the time. The Manorial system tended to keep the majority of people tied to the land and to the ancestral estates to which many of them had been born. Towns and even cities were beginning to develop, but not on any grand scale. In the 12th- century English kings also had significant holdings in France, particularly around Calais. This meant they also had a financial stake in the finished cloth markets so there probably wasn't any real incentive during the reigns of the Norman kings of England to disrupt the status quo.

Of course sheep production, as well as cloth making, were never restricted to Britain and Flanders. Sheep were being raised and cloth produced almost everywhere. The first tentative steps of what would be an extremely prosperous Italian cloth trade began to be taken during the 12th century, whilst many sheep were also being raised in Spain, though not with the quality of wool for which the Iberian Peninsula would eventually become famous.

In 1216 King Henry III came to the throne of England. There were problems between England and France in the early part of Henry's reign – a foretaste of thing to come. Henry III had been only nine years of age when he ascended the throne and it took, on and off, until 1259 for the animosity between the two nations to subside. When it did, Henry started to have significant problems in his own back yard. His penchant for 'favourites' incensed the powerful barons of England, who felt that he was governing without taking account of their opinions and therefore working against their best interests. For a while he was taken prisoner but was reinstated as king in 1265. Henceforth he moderated the nature of his rule and he did take greater notice of the barons. One of his measures, in 1270, just two years before his death, was to cordially invite wool spinners and weavers from Flanders to start a new life in England. This was the beginning of a process that would go on for several centuries and the first documented Royal recognition of the importance of wool to the developing English economy. Some of Henry's courtiers had been supporting English cloth production for longer. Back in 1258, one of the great English magnates, Simon de Montfort, spoke out against such large exports of raw wool. Montfort was the baron who had taken the king prisoner and in 1258 he convened a great Council. This ordered that England's wool should be worked at home rather than being taken abroad and it further advocated that 'everyone within the realm should wear woollen cloth made in this country'.

Henry III's son, Edward I, spent a great deal of his reign between 1239 and 1307 fighting, and for a while was daggers-drawn with the French Crown. Towards the end of the 12th century the French throne was occupied by Philip IV, a man who had just as high an opinion of himself as did Edward. The two came to blows over the region of Gascony. England was not anywhere near as powerful as France at the time and Edward expended significant effort in trying to line up allies on the Continent. In particular he paid great attention to Flanders, which because of the wool trade was a natural friend of England.

Some recognition of the importance of English woollen cloth emerged during Edward's reign. In the midst of his foreign troubles and in need of cash, in 1297 Edward ordered his officials to seize all wool in the realm that belonged to foreigners and to sell it. The money flowed into his own coffers but the officers who had carried out his orders had been rather too diligent and had taken wool that belonged to English merchants. This turned out to be the least of the problems because in 1294 Parliament had granted to Edward the right to tax all wool leaving the ports of England. The King had secured large loans from Italian bankers and by 1297 they were snapping at his heels for payment. He told the country that his powers to tax wool were still in operation but the English Parliament was furious because it saw in Edward's actions a violation of Magna Carta. This was a great charter that the barons had forced King John to sign in 1215. According to the charter taxes could only be levied with the agreement of the community of the realm, which meant Parliament.

Later in the same year Edward was forced by the barons to cancel the tax on wool but he had thought up a ruse to put money directly into the Royal coffers and it would not be forgotten by his successors. For generations, kings of England would draw a large part of their income from taxes on wool.

Edward died in 1307, leaving behind his much less able son, Edward II, but he passed away whilst Philip IV was still on the throne of France. The actions of Philip in the later years of his own reign would ensure that England and France would be at each other's throats for decades but he would also unknowingly begin a process that would set the seal on Britain's ultimate greatness.

Kings at war

King Philip IV of France was also known as Philip the Fair. This had nothing whatsoever to do with his propensity for being even-handed in his dealings with the world at large. The word 'fair' in this context is a translation of the French 'belle' which relates to Philip's looks, rather than his nature. Philip IV was grasping, greedy, cruel, suspicious and naturally tyrannical – in effect he was quite typical of the kings of his period. However, whilst some monarchs were at least willing to listen to wise councils Philip hardly ever did. Looked at with hindsight his long reign probably did more to damage his country than that of almost any other monarch in the history of France.

Philip seems to have been pathologically incapable of co-operating with other kings and princes in the Europe of his day and in particular harboured a deep hatred of England. He was also very suspicious regarding the Knights Templar, who by the end of the 13th century had grown colossally rich and very powerful. Fate provided him with a means of getting rid of the Templars, even if England represented a more difficult problem. As a result of a judicious marriage, the region of Champagne, where the Templar headquarters lay, came into Philip's hands at the start of the 14th century. By this time the Champagne fairs were justifiably the most famous merchant markets in Europe. They attracted people from all over the continent and from far beyond and made Champagne very wealthy.

Not only did Philip move against the Templars in 1307, accusing them of every crime imaginable, his disastrous foreign policy also lead to an immediate and rapid decline in the Champagne fairs. Destroying the Templars, at least in France, wasn't all that difficult. Philip had an important ally in the form of his childhood friend Bertrand de Got, who had been elected to the papacy as Clement V. Philip 'persuaded' Clement to dissolve the order and its last Grand Master, Jacques de Molay, was burned alive in Paris a few years later. What Philip had actually managed to achieve, though he would never know it, was to start a revolution in trade that would eventually lead to the destruction of the feudal state and the end of the power of the Catholic Church.

The Templars had represented the biggest single, cohesive banking and shipping organisation in the world. The order had become like a multinational company and had branches everywhere. Neither Philip nor the Pope could get rid of them all. Despite the fact that the Pope excommunicated all Templars and instructed their land to be confiscated across the whole of Christendom, some countries, such as Portugal, were unwilling to move against the Templars. As a result the order simply changed its name in Portugal and carried on much as before. Meanwhile in Germany the Templars had become so powerful and so deeply enmeshed in the running of society that nobody dared to move against them at all.

Where Templar influence was lost, in France, Italy and around the Mediterranean, new agencies flowed in to fill the vacuum. In particular this was the time when banking institutions in Northern Italy began to gain ground. Putting an end to the Templars as an accepted institution did nothing to destroy trade – it merely put more of it into the hands of secular agencies.

Philip's foreign policies turned out to be both ill considered and counterproductive. Not content with fighting a protracted war with England over disputed lands in France, he also chose to interfere in the running of Flanders. In 1299 he aided the disgruntled citizens of Flanders in a struggle against their much-hated Count, Guy of Dampierre, but as soon as the Count had been overthrown in 1300, Philip declared that Flanders was now French. The Flemings, always a passionately independent breed, disagreed. They rose up against Philip and at first defeated him in the disastrous Battle of Courtrai in 1302. Philip retaliated and though he did defeat the Flemmings in 1304, he was eventually forced to give them a much higher degree of independence than he would have wished. Unfortunately for all concerned this period of uncertainty and war in Flanders seriously damaged the woollen textile trade. Although in coming years it would recover somewhat, the Champagne fairs had also been mortally wounded and other markets for finished cloth began to be established.

In England the reign of Edward I, who had been a very powerful king, was followed by that of his son Edward II, who was weak in comparison, though his time on the throne did mark something of a watershed in the realisation that the woollen cloth producing regions of England were important and should be supported. In 1326, just a year before his death he issued a declaration. This stated that: *'No cloth which is manufactured outside England, Ireland and Wales can be bought in this country, except by kings, queens, earls, barons, knights, ladies and their legitimate children, archbishops, bishops, and others who spend £40 a year on their rents'*. Since £40 per year was a huge sum at the time, the ban included almost everyone. His edict doesn't seem to have had the required effect because although English cloth production was increasing, Flemish woollens remained very popular and were still imported in large quantities.

One of the most influential of the English kings of the period, Edward III, came to the throne in 1327. He was a capable leader but just as warlike as his grandfather had been. In 1340, as a result of dynastic complications and previous wars, Edward assumed the title of King of France. The French nobility were not at all happy with this state of affairs and what followed was an extremely protracted series of battles between the two nations that are now referred to as the Hundred Years War. Edward and his son, the Black Prince, captured extensive lands in France and like other kings before him, Edward could not resist interfering in the running of Flanders. As early as 1336 he had forbidden the export of English wool to Flanders. This was a political move, intended to force the Flemmings to back him in his dispute with France.

With no other reliable source of raw wool Flanders suffered terribly. Many of its citizens starved and it was not until 1338 that Edward once again allowed wool to be exported to the region. At the same time he was engaged in trying to support the home woollen textile industry. Even before the blockade, in 1331, he had issued letters of protection to Flemish weavers who wished to travel to England to live and work. He promised that they would feed on beef and mutton and that they would have comfortable beds. He even suggested that the richest yeomen in England would offer their daughters in marriage to the Flemmings. As another and very significant gesture to the woollen trade in England Edward ordered that the Lord Chancellor, the most powerful individual in Parliament, would henceforth sit on a woolsack whilst presiding over the House of Lords. This tradition has persisted until the present day.

English wool remained as popular as ever and was recognised at this time as being probably the best available anywhere in Europe. This was especially true of the wool from Cotswold sheep, which sold for significant sums on the open market.

Like the kings before him Edward III was not slow in realising what all the exported English wool could mean to him financially. By the time of his reign Parliament was already developing some muscle. Money needed to fight wars, especially against the French, had to be voted to the King by Parliament, which wasn't always particularly willing to play ball. The three estates of the realm represented in Parliament were the nobility, the clergy and the commons. However, a growing section of society lay outside the remit of established Parliament. This was the merchant class. Edward worked out deals with them that meant he could tax the export of raw wool without reference to Parliament. In 1336 he held a series of Merchant Assemblies, at which the level of taxation on wool was agreed. It was decided that every sack of wool would be taxed at 20 shillings, with an equal loan being offered to the King by the merchants on each sack. This deal circumnavigated Parliament and put the massive amounts of money raised straight into the coffers of the King himself.

By 1351 circumstances had changed because many wool merchants had gone bankrupt thanks to Edward's meddling. Parliament finally brought the King to heel and it was declared that henceforth any deal undertaken between the monarch and the merchants without Parliamentary approval would be illegal. Not that this stopped Edward from interfering and trying to raise more revenue, but his efforts were, in the main, unsuccessful.

In between the first meetings of the Merchant Assemblies and the King being brought to book in 1351, Edward's realm, together with the rest of Europe, had suffered one of the greatest disasters ever to strike humanity. It was the called the Black Death.

The Black Death probably came from Asia and is thought to have been a particularly virulent strain of bubonic plague. It began in Europe in 1347 and raced across countries at a terrifying pace. Bubonic plague was passed directly from victim to victim but could also be caught as a result of bites from fleas that had themselves become diseased. The fleas had bitten rats that already carried the contagion. The Black Death arrived in England in 1348, by which time it was already ravaging populations throughout Europe.

It is thought that up to 50% of Europe's population was destroyed during the epidemic. The Black Death was no respecter of rank or position so the aristocracy, the clergy, merchants and commoners all suffered a similar fate. Those struck down became covered in black, festering sores. They generally died within a couple of days and things became so bad that there were no longer enough people alive to tend to the sick or to bury the dead. On occasions whole communities were wiped out, or left so depleted that they were abandoned. The horror and terror of the Black Death cannot be underestimated. There was no understanding of what the disease was, or even how it was spread and right up until the 20th century bubonic plague defied any form of treatment.

It terms of the woollen trade the Black Death did as much to kill potential buyers of cloth as it did to exterminate those involved in its manufacture, so the two situations balanced each other out. But it was the lasting effect of the contagion, particularly in England, that would eventually lead to a complete reordering of society.

The most important contribution the Black Death made to the restructuring of everyday life was that it virtually destroyed feudalism at a stroke. Peasants who had been willing to work on their lord's land with no financial gain suddenly found themselves in great demand. They moved about from one manor to another, seeking out the best wages and taking on a level of personal choice and freedom that had never been available to them before. In England the Government did all it could to try and force labourers to stay on their manors and to accept a livelihood that was pegged at a pre-plague level, but it was to no avail.

Another effect of the Black Death was to create a class of yeoman farmer that had not existed to any great extent before. Individuals who managed to survive the disease but whose families had been destroyed, found themselves much better off as a result of inheritance. This was fine but what use was more land if there was nobody available to tend it? The old system of strip farming which had been so inefficient began to disappear rapidly. What seems to have happened in many cases is that those who had come to inherit many strips of land from family members who had been wiped out by the plague began to swap strips with other benefactors, until they achieved larger plots of land that were much more productive. The old strips had been divided by mounds, which wasted useable earth, and in any case larger plots naturally provided economy of scale. The population soon recovered and people had to be fed. The old way of farming was suddenly seen to be desperately inefficient and it was at this point in history that the Cistercian system of enlarging plots of land and then enclosing them appeared to be the way forward.

Old structures in society, like the manors, soon began to fall apart. So disastrous had the Black Death been to the clergy that the Church was forced to take on new priests who were far less educated than had been the case before. Paradoxically, although the plague had initially been seen as a scourge sent by God, in the end it also resulted in widespread religious reform, even if this took a century or two to show itself. The world of almost everyone across Europe would never be the same again and it didn't matter how much monarchs tried to redress the balance, society was changed forever. It is a sad reflection on the implications of the disease that the Cistercians, whose methods of farming and manufacture would offer so much to future generations, were themselves effectively destroyed by the Black Death. Their abbeys remained but they became a shadow of what they had been. The system of lay brothers fell apart completely and the Cistercians were forced to rent out land to tenant farmers.

The reign of Richard II of England saw a major repercussion of the Black Death. In 1381 vast numbers of people, especially in the south of England, rose up against what they saw as unjust rule. This incident is now popularly known as the Peasants Revolt. A bedraggled, makeshift army of thousands marched on London, killing the Archbishop of Canterbury and other notable figures and they assembled at Smithfield, where the young King Richard, then only fourteen years of age, agreed to meet their leaders. The main grievance had been the imposition of a Poll Tax, which represented an entirely different form of taxation in England. It demanded a yearly payment of one shilling per adult, mainly to pay for continuing wars with France. The peasants saw this as both unjust and impossible. The young King made all sorts of promises in order to convince the assembly to disperse and though he went back on most of what he had offered, the writing was on the wall for a society in England that had lasted since at least the Norman Conquest.

Quite soon Parliament was passing laws forbidding people to wear clothes that were 'above their station'. This is an indication that many of the undisputed rules of society, through which the masses had been kept in their place, were failing. Chaucer's *Canterbury Tales*, written in 1476, is the story of a group of pilgrims on their way to the shrine of St Thomas Becket in Canterbury. The pilgrims are drawn from every strata of society but it is clear from Chaucer's description of the clothes worn by the humblest of the pilgrims that rules regarding dress had broken down completely by the second half of the 15th century.[19] Bright colours

---

19 *The Canterbury Tales*, Penguin Classics, Chaucer, Penguin Books, London 1996

became popular, which would once have been unthinkable for the lower orders, whilst rich merchants even began to wear cloth of gold, which had been reserved for royalty and aristocracy.

Despite the difficulties of the period, both woollen exports and cloth manufacture in England, as well as other parts of Britain, were going from strength to strength. In the aftermath of the Black Death more people were travelling in from the countryside to take up life in the towns. York in particular became an important centre of woollen cloth production, but it was not as prosperous as the Cotswolds and the West Country generally, partly because of the huge flocks of sheep in the area, the wool of which was readily available and of extremely high quality.

In terms of producing woollen cloth, what was just as important as a readily available workforce was the right sort of water. Raw wool had to be cleaned and this was achieved best in 'soft' water. In many locations watercourses run through lime-rich strata. As a result the water becomes rich in calcium, magnesium and other minerals and this prevents an adequate 'scouring' of the wool.

Scouring is the first process in the sequence between raw wool and finished cloth. Wool straight from the back of a sheep is generally very dirty and replete with small twigs and bits of vegetation. It is also rich in lanolin, a natural fat that helps to keep the sheep dry. All of the accumulated dirt and a fair proportion of the lanolin must be removed before the wool can pass on to the next process. This isn't as easy as it sounds because the wool at this stage is quite vulnerable. Too much agitation and the fibres of the wool can become entangled or else compressed, which is known as 'felting'. Detergent helps the process these days but historically speaking this was not available commercially, though plant extracts and some minerals would have been used. For example a common weed in Britain bears the name 'Soapwort', (*Saponaria officinalis*) testimony to the fact that the plant was once used in the scouring of wool. With such primitive detergents it was critical that the water used was low in lime, in order that a good lather could be achieved. Lime prevents this and makes scouring virtually impossible.

A number of factors dictated whether a given area of England, and indeed Britain as a whole, would turn out to be ideal for not only the breeding and raising of sheep but also for the creation of finished woollen cloth and amongst these factors water was top of the list. As an example, parts of North Yorkshire and in particular the Yorkshire Dales have always been important areas for breeding and raising sheep, but only some of these dales or valleys turned out to be centres of woollen cloth production. In much of the area covered by the Northern Dales there are significant areas of limestone, making the water unsuitable. Further south, and particularly in Airedale, the water is softer and this region eventually became the heart of the English woollen textile industry.

In addition the towns that first proved to be important to the woollen textile trade had to have good communications with surrounding areas, and in particular with the coast or a navigable river. Overland transport was difficult and expensive, both for the movement of raw wool and for the finished cloth. Up until the 18th century and more recently in remoter areas, roads were virtually nonexistent or were so rough as to be unusable in the winter months. A further requirement was sufficient people because woollen textile production was very labour intensive until the 19th century. As a result an area with a steady reliable workforce was a must.

The ideal situation was a place close to where the sheep were being reared, so that the raw wool did not have to travel too far, and a location that was accessible to a port. In addition it had to have a good all-year soft water supply and sufficient workers in the vicinity. These requirements came together well in areas around Bristol, towns close to Salisbury Plain, some locations in East Anglia and in and around York. Woollen cloth was also being produced in Wales, Scotland and Ireland by the 14th century but not on so large a scale as that in England.

Just as had taken place in Flanders, the Woollen Guilds began to have a great bearing on the production and sale of English cloth. One such was The Drapers Company, or more properly, 'The Master and Wardens and Brethren and Sisters of the Guild or Fraternity of the Blessed Virgin Mary of the Mystery of Drapers of the City of London'. This was formed in 1180 and by the time of the reign of Richard III was already very rich and powerful. The Drapers Company was originally restricted to dealings in woollen cloth and its members had much to do with the formation of the Staples. The Staples were ports and towns where English wool could be sold. They were important because if the export of wool went unregulated, the sacks of wool could not be taxed. As we have seen the tax on wool represented an important component of Royal revenues. The first Staple port had been Antwerp, but eventually twelve English Staple towns were established before finally the Staple passed to Calais.[20]

Also in existence in London, from at least the 12th century was the Weaver's Company, which represented the most skilful of the crafts within woollen textile manufacture. The companies and guilds remained powerful institutions that tried to prevent anyone outside of their own structure taking up a profession that threatened their own monopoly. In Flanders there had been regular periods of disorder when armed thugs hired by the guilds in the cities had attacked small-time woollen production in villages and country areas.

Wherever woollen textiles were made, the processes involved were broadly similar. Once the wool had been scoured and then dried, it had to be carded. This process was crucial because it straightened out the fibres of the wool. In its raw state the fibres of wool go in every possible direction and this makes it impossible to spin. Carding, originally undertaken by hand with the use of special combs, forces the fibres to go in the same direction. Carding combs similar to the ones used for centuries are still available for home producers and a picture of a set is shown below.

The carded wool now went to be spun. Originally this was undertaken using simple drop spindles, such as that mentioned and shown in Chapter 2. This was a laborious and time-consuming process. By the late Middle Ages, probably during the 14th century, a much better device was starting to appear across Europe. This was the spinning wheel. Its origins are obscure though most experts

---

20 *The New Draperies in the Low Countries and England*, 1300-1800, Editor Negley Harte, Oxford University Press, 1998

think it came from India. The spinning wheel takes much of the work out of turning the fibres of the raw, carded wool into useable yarn. Simple spinning wheels are invariably operated via a treadle that turns a large wheel and the wheel is connected to a rotating bobbin by way of an endless cord. Carded wool is fed to the bobbin and a combination of the hand movements of the person spinning and the machine itself twists the fibres and then winds them onto the bobbin. Spinning wheels have various devices that dictate the tightness of the finished yarn and they also have gearing that allows the spinning wheel to run at different speeds.

A pair of traditional carding combs

A typical Saxony type spinning wheel (courtesy of Wyatt Spinning Wheels)

The use of spinning wheels was the first in a series of processes that made textile production much quicker. It also formed part of the earliest cottage industry upon which early woollen cloth manufacture depended. Before spinning wheels were used it would have taken many days or even weeks for one spinner in a family to produce sufficient yarn to make even a small length of cloth. As a result the adoption of the spinning wheel represented an absolute revolution in its day.

The spinning wheel also changed working circumstances in another way. Although the spinning wheel is a fairly primitive device by the standards of today's spinning techniques, its purchase still lay beyond the financial wherewithal of the poor. This was a problem because these were the very people who were creating the yarn for the looms. In many cases where textile production existed within towns, small factories began to emerge, where people would go to do their spinning. There the wheels belonged to the owners of the establishments and the workers were paid a wage. Where spinning was undertaken in more remote areas, local woollen merchants began to appear. They would often 'lend' a spinning machine to a given family, also supplying them with fleece and collecting the spun yarn.

The yarn was sometimes dyed at this stage, particularly if the textile carried patterns woven into the cloth – hence the expression 'dyed in the wool'. It was then passed to the loom, where the real business of making the 'piece' as the finished length was known, took place.

By the 14th century looms had become moderately sophisticated. The vertical loom, in use since Stone Age times, had disappeared, and had been replaced with a flat bed loom, usually referred to as a 'handloom'.

A typical handloom from a painting by A. W. Bayes

At its simplest the handloom is a device that allows the various threads of the warp to be separated so that a shuttle containing the weft can be passed back and forth between the warp. The use of pedals allows the warp to be reset after each passage of the shuttle, so that the desired weave can be achieved. The weave is gradually built up in this way and the loom also has a device that allows the weft to be compressed, so that the finished weave is not too loose. More advanced handlooms also had devices, worked by pedals, that allowed simple patterns to be made in the cloth.

The problem with the hand loom lay partly in the time it took to weave cloth, mainly because the shuttle had to be passed beneath the warp threads manually (through a gap known as the shed). This also restricted the width of the finished cloth because the dependent factor was the physical reach of the weaver. It may have been partly for this reason that weaving became an essentially male preserve. Men tend to be taller and so have a longer reach than women.

Once the woollen piece had been woven it went to be dyed if that process had not already been undertaken, and then one of the most important processes of all was necessary. This was known as 'fulling'. No matter how good the weave, it would still be looser than was commercially desirable. Fulling the cloth compacted the threads, as well as cleaning the finished cloth. Originally this was a laborious process that was none too pleasant. The woven piece was placed in a large vat. Onto it was poured a mixture of water, a chemical known as 'Fullers Earth' and human urine. This was then walked on for long periods of time before a sufficient compactness was achieved.

Fulling was a time-consuming business until fulling mills were invented. These came into use as early as the 13th century in some places and were widespread by the 15th century. They represented the real start of mechanisation in the woollen textile trade but they could not be located just anywhere. In other words the cloth had to be taken to them. Fulling mills or stocks were very large wooden hammers, operated by water wheels. They pounded the cloth continually and did a much better job of compacting and cleaning the cloth but they were entirely dependent on a sufficiently strong stream of water being available.

Once the cloth had been fulled and then rinsed, it was taken outside to be placed along a series of posts known as 'tenters'. There it was left to dry. The piece was held in place by hooks that sometimes came adrift in the wind. This led to the modern expression 'being on tenterhooks'.

Further processes were necessary in some cases, for example 'raising'. The surface of the finished cloth was hard and if a softer texture was required, which was usually the case, it was necessary to make the cloth more comfortable to the wearer by teasing out the fibres on its surface. This was known as 'raising the nap' and was undertaken using one of nature's gifts – a flower head called 'a teasel'. The plant in question, *Dipsacus sylvestris*, has a very spiny rosette, which when dried is ideal for raising the nap on wool. It has been used for this purpose since at least the 15th century and probably earlier.

In the early days of cloth making the teasels were mounted onto a handle and used manually to raise the surface of the cloth.

Teasels mounted on a handle

A very skilled task followed the teasing of the cloth and this was known as 'shearing'. The raised fibres had to be cut back so that they were all of a uniform length. This was achieved by the use of a very heavy set of metal shears. Before shearing became a mechanised process, those who undertook the task were very well paid because of the long period it took to train for the task.

After being pressed the finished piece was now ready for sale and was passed onto the merchant, for domestic sale or to be exported.

By the 15th century this process of producing finished cloth was being undertaken in numerous locations throughout the whole of the British Isles, though that did not mean that Britain had achieved a monopoly on finished woollen production. On the contrary, Flanders was still turning out hundreds of thousands of woollen pieces each year, whilst another contender was gaining ground rapidly.

Woollen textile manufacture would ultimately be responsible for the biggest change in European attitudes that would ever take place. However, this process did not happen in Britain at all but rather in Italy and in particular in the city of Florence.

Wool men, bankers and reformers

At the same time as woollen textile manufacture was becoming established within Britain, and especially England, the main area of woollen textile production within Europe remained Flanders. However, down in the Mediterranean there was another contender for the creation of the finished cloth that both Europe and the East were anxious to buy. This was Italy, where woollen production had been going on in a number of places. None of these would turn out to be nearly as important as the City State of Florence.

Florence is situated in Northern Italy, a good way inland from the Ligurian Sea, in fact almost central, and without port facilities of its own. It was already a significant location during Roman times. Partly for reasons of defence Roman Florence was situated on the confluence of two streams, the Arno and the Mugnone and it was also fortified from a very early date. The region flourished during the Roman period but fell onto harder times during the Byzantine and Lombard period, when the area was subject to barbarian invasion. By the time of the Emperor Charlemagne, Florence became a county of the Holy Roman Empire and was subjected to a feudal economy, not unlike that prevailing in England and France.

During the 11th century Florence became of great significance to a most remarkable woman. Her name was Matilda and after the death of her mother and husband she became the sole countess of Tuscany. This put her directly in control of Florence. Matilda was a strong supporter of the Pope but because of the politics of the time this brought her into open conflict with the Holy Roman Emperor. The forces of the Emperor besieged Florence in 1082 but because of the organised nature of the city fathers and their defences, the siege failed.

Matilda died in 1115 but she left behind her the legacy of what Florence would eventually become. She had granted wide-ranging powers to the citizens themselves and upon her death Florence became essentially democratic, something unheard of up to that period. In 1138 there was a meeting of the Tuscan cities and it was decided to form a league between them. It was at this meeting that Florence first actually referred to itself as 'a commune'. Florence had come to be ruled by a committee of citizens that included both religious and secular representatives. There was some interference from outside agencies in the years that followed but in the main Florence was left alone to get on with its experiment in self-government. As a result it began to flourish. By 1172 the city was doing so well that its protective walls were much enlarged. The rise of mercantile activity was startling and some of the merchants who were achieving the most at this time were taking lessons in credit transactions and banking from the Knights Templar.

By the start of the 13th century Florence and the surrounding region was already developing a good reputation as an area that produced high quality woollen cloth. In addition to buying in large quantities of raw wool, much of which came from Britain, the Florentines were particularly good at 'finishing'. This involved importing ready-woven cloth, most specifically from Flanders. The rough cloth was fulled, dyed and finished within Florence and then sold on into the city's growing international markets. Florence grew stronger and was soon dealing in all other manner of commodities but wool remained paramount to its organisation and economy.

Although the city became a sort of democracy, the various guilds were the guiding force behind its success. The largest of these was the 'Arte Della Lana' or the wool guild. Throughout the whole of the 13th and much of the 14th century this guild was the most powerful and influential of all the institutions of Florence. Its headquarters were situated in the city itself and from there the Arte Della Lana supervised everyone associated with woollen cloth production and its associated skills. Probably the most important fact was that Florence was self-ruled and so could legislate to produce the very best quality of product right across the board. As a result Florentine cloth became famous throughout the known world. It sold well and the profits were ploughed back into the city, where specific families began to grow extremely rich.

No family was more influential to Florence than that of the Medici. Part of the eventual success of the Medici lay in the fact that it was a family that had risen not from the nobility but from the patrician class. Because of their origins the Medici were popular with the ordinary people of Florence who repeatedly supported Medici family members in the running of the city. [21]

Right from the start Medici interests lay primarily in wool. The family had once been small-time woollen cloth producers but with judicious marriages and a shrewd business sense they eventually became financers and then outright bankers. Despite their elevated position the Medici showed great concern for the disenfranchised 'Ciompi', which although a name given to that class of workers who had no direct representation, actually referred specifically to the wool carders. In 1378 there was a revolt of Ciompi, which for a brief time brought the most complete degree of democracy to Florence that the world had known until that time. The experiment did not last long and the old guard eventually predominated but it was enough to ensure that the authorities in Florence always kept a weather eye on the lower classes and their needs.

Savestro de Medici, who had participated in the revolt of the Ciompi, was eventually banished from Florence in 1383 and this led to an early slump in the fortunes of the family but the later Giovanni Bicci de Medici rebuilt the family's wealth. Once again this was achieved primarily as a result of wool. The Medici became the richest family in Italy and most probably in Europe. Giovanni was followed by his son Cosimo de Medici who by 1434 single-handedly controlled the government of Florence. Although banished for

---

21   *The Medici: Godfathers of the Renaissance*, Paul Strathern, Pimlico, London, 2004

a short time as a result of resistance from another wealthy family, the Albizzi, Cosimo eventually returned to Florence, where he was very popular with the masses. Cosimo was the first of the Medici to spend lavishly on artistic works, making Florence one of the most beautiful cities in Europe.

Lorenzo de Medici was Cosimo's second son and he would become the most famous Medici of all, eventually being known as Lorenzo the Magnificent. The list of Lorenzo's accomplishments is incredible. He was extremely well educated and intelligent – a just ruler and a great patron of the arts. Creating libraries that contained not just religious but also secular works, the Medici began to attract many of the 'thinkers' of Europe, whose interests lay as much in Classical history as in their commitment to the Church. They established universities where it was possible to study subjects other than religion and they encouraged a degree of radical free-thinking that would have been completely unacceptable elsewhere. Other cities in Italy soon followed suit and what followed is recognised as being one of the most important periods in the history of Europe. Amongst other things it would lead to changes in religious practice, a rise in the importance of science and to a severe lessening of the influence of the Roman Catholic Church. This period is known as the Renaissance.

It is probable that the Vatican itself would have looked unfavourably on what was happening in Florence, were it not for the fact that successive popes came to rely more and more on the Medici. As a result the Medici ultimately helped to destroy the power of the Catholic Church, even if this had not been its direct intention.

Many analysts accept that the 'Enlightenment' that took place in Europe during the 18th century, and the subsequent appearance of massive international trade and capitalism, was the creation of the new Protestant version of Christianity. It now looks as if this model is far too simplistic. There was a time when the Church owned huge areas of land across Europe and every Christian was subject to religious taxes, known as tithes. Understandably the Vatican wanted its share of the Church money forthcoming from society, made available for its use in a currency it understood and used – this was the ducket. Originally the tithes from England had been collected by the Knights Templar, which found means to help itself on the way. Because of England's utter dependence on wool, which was as good as a currency in any case, England's tithes were paid in sacks of wool. These were traded by the Templars and turned into the currency the Vatican preferred. The Vatican also did well out of these transactions because in between the tithe payment and the arrival of the duckets into the Vatican coffers, the money was working and growing, mainly as a result of interest charged on money lent to merchants, individuals and even kings.

Some of these loans attracted interest as great as 60% and they definitely contravened canon law, which did not allow interest to be charged. The Vatican knew very well what was going on but it did not want to kill the goose that was laying so many golden eggs and so it kept quiet.

In their book '*Merchant and Money Men*',[22] authors F. and G. Gies readily admit that the Vatican was a leading agency in proto-capitalism for quite some time prior to the Renaissance and the religious Reformation that followed.

After the Templars had disappeared the Medici became the Vatican's bankers and continued to manage Rome's money in much the same way. With the permission of the Vatican the Medici used its money to invest in a range of ventures. Originally most of these were associated with wool but that situation soon changed as Florence became more powerful and increased its contacts overseas.

At every stage successive popes saw good dividends coming in on their investments. They were satisfied with this situation because the Medici were after all only using money that was lying around until it was needed for some specific purpose. What Rome didn't see, or more likely did not understand, was that all the commerce and the international trade was changing the nature of Europe. What is more the Medici and other rich merchants and bankers in Florence and the other leading cities of Italy were spreading a form of enlightenment that was separating people from the authority of

---

22 *Merchant and Money Men*, F & G Gies, Redwood Publishing, 1972

the Church. Florence was not the only important city in Italy. It was rivalled by places such as Venice, Rome itself and Milan, but its influence had come early and it was more closely tied to the finances of the Vatican than any other city. There is no doubt that its affluence and power was a direct consequence of its early and lasting trade in woollen cloth.

With more and more money rolling in, the popes of the period became huge spenders. More to the point they became much less spiritually motivated and they were drawn in the main from the leading families of Italy, including the Medici itself. Matters came to a head when the popes spent so much money that even their resources began to dwindle. In an effort to refill their diminished coffers they turned to practices that would cause revulsion and revolution beyond Italy. In particular they began to sell indulgences, which meant that for a specific payment anyone could literally 'buy' their way into heaven. This ingenious if morally corrupt strategy made the popes rich again but it would backfire on them in ways they never expected.

Led by a series of reformist zealots, the most famous of whom was a German by the name of Martin Luther, priests themselves began to rebel against the practices of the Church. Had the leaders in Rome taken notice of what was happening and done something to put the situation right all could have been well. Rather they reacted violently to the radicals, forcing them to split with the Catholic Church and to form new denominations. Once started this 'reformation' spread across Europe like a rash and was especially strong in Germany and Flanders. By the 16th century the scene was set for some of the most vicious and bloody wars Europe would ever see.

The reformed Catholics became known as Protestants. They refused to return to the old ways of worshiping and developed a hatred for Rome and Catholicism, the effects of which are still to be seen in the world today. The Reformation would ultimately lead directly to the greatness of Britain but more as a result of events taking place elsewhere rather than because of what was happening amongst the religious adherents of Britain itself. A major factor was the upheaval that began to take place in Flanders, England's biggest rival in the production of woollen cloth.

For many years Flanders had fallen under the direct rule of the House of Burgundy. There had been problems but these had generally been kept to a minimum and the region remained economically strong. Early in the 16th century the Dukedom of Burgundy passed to Charles V, who was not only the son of Philip, Duke of Burgundy, but also a direct descendent of the House of Hapsburg. As a result he came to rule over such a wide area that it was said that 'the sun never set on his empire'. Soon he was King of Castile in Spain and more to the point he was a devout Catholic. He moved against the Protestants in his domains in Flanders and by so doing added to the religious carnage that was breaking out in so many places. Flanders was eventually ravaged as a result and was so badly damaged that its economic position was lost forever. Cloth making was badly hit for a number of reasons. Chief amongst these was the relocation of the much of the population.

Around the same period England had problems of its own. By 1509 the country had a new king. He was Henry VIII, an astute and intelligent man with very definite ideas about how his domains should be ruled. Unfortunately for Henry he gradually became fixated on one specific problem. No matter how many healthy sons he fathered to his many mistresses, his Queen, Katherine of Aragon, could only produce a single daughter. As a result and desperate for a male heir, Henry sought an annulment of his marriage but Katherine had powerful relatives and the Pope would not dissolve the union. Henry was given to fits of fury and indignation and such was his anger at the attitude of the Pope he eventually took the decision to split with Rome and to create the Church of England. This wasn't exactly a reformation of the sort that was taking place across many areas in Europe because Henry still considered himself to be a Catholic. However, with the passing of time the English would become every bit as Protestant as their neighbours in Flanders.

Henry eventually got his divorce, though not with the Pope's blessing. By so doing he angered Spain, from which Katherine of Aragon originated. New lines were being drawn in the sand and

England found itself naturally supported by, and in turn supporting, the waves of reformation elsewhere. Cloth makers in Flanders were finding it increasingly difficult not only to spin and weave but merely to stay alive. Many of them felt there was nothing else to do except to move to a more favourable place and for more than one reason this invariably meant England.

Within the confines of Henry's kingdom the Flemmings would be safe in a religious sense and they would also be able to continue doing what they understood the best – making cloth. The trickle of Flemmings that had been flowing into England since the Norman Conquest suddenly became a raging torrent. Since England, and in fact most of Britain, found its markets for raw wool in Europe much diminished, it was natural that a greater degree of finished textile production would take place at home. There were still a significant number of places to which the finished cloth could be exported. Not only was Antwerp still flourishing, feeding the traditional markets in Western Central Europe, but England was also having a great deal of success selling its cloth into German, Baltic and even Russian markets.

It was at this time that England and Spain began to form a bitter rivalry that would last for centuries. This was not simply a response to a difference in religious practices and actually had far more to do with trade and influence. During the 15th century what had been a divided Spain gradually became united. The marriage in 1469 between Ferdinand of Aragon and Isabella of Castile greatly aided the process and by 1492 the last of the Muslims had been thrown out of Southern Spain. With cohesion came prosperity and the development of an industry that had been taking place across areas of the Iberian Peninsula for a long time, namely the rearing of sheep.

Spanish wool had been used for decades before this period, especially in Flanders. But the wool was of an inferior quality and it had to be carefully mixed with the longer staple English wool in order to be suitable. Using a mixture of their own sheep, together with strains bred and improved by the Muslim Moors, the Spanish eventually arrived at a better sheep than any yet produced elsewhere.

It was the direct ancestor of an animal that had existed since the days of the Roman Emperor Claudius, but it had been refined to such a degree by the 15th century that its wool was of the finest quality available anywhere. This was the famous Merino sheep, upon which most of the major wool producing flocks of the world are now based.

England was still exporting vast amounts of wool prior to Henry VIII's split with Rome and the difficulties that were being caused by the Spanish possession of Flanders. Better Spanish fleeces threatened this monopoly. This fact, together with the religious differences and the expansionist policies of both Spain and England, set the seal on an animosity that knew no bounds. The result of the power struggle would not simply play itself out on European soil but across the rapidly expanding world of the 16th century.

England turned upside down

Henry VIII of England divorced his former wife, Katherine of Aragon in 1533 and promptly married his new queen, Anne Boleyn. It is still generally trotted out by historians that Henry took this step just because he so badly needed a male heir, and although this is part of the reason, there were other important factors that led to his actions. In order to divorce Katherine, Henry had to make a formalised break with Rome, not just for himself but on behalf of his country. This would mean excommunication and the formal opposition of other European Catholic states, including France and Spain. It is very unlikely that the King would have taken such a serious step simply to continue his dynasty, no matter how important that may have been to him.

The truth of the matter is that Henry was rapidly running out of money. His father, Henry VII, had been miserly to a fault. He had also been an extremely judicious ruler – at least as far as the exchequer was concerned. As a result Henry VIII had inherited a very prosperous kingdom when he came to the throne in 1509. Almost from the moment he put on the royal crown Henry junior began to spend as if there was no tomorrow. He loved fine buildings, wonderful clothes, pageantry and splendour and in any case felt it was only right that he should be seen to rival the awesome wealth of the French kings.

The result was that by the late 1520s he was, at least in royal terms, as poor as a church mouse. The excesses of the Vatican and the

way it was bleeding every last penny from believers across Europe
was as unpopular in England as it was anywhere else in Europe
and Henry judged the mood of the times very well. England was
studded with very rich abbeys, which had been building up their
wealth over three hundred years or more. Orders such as that of
the Cistercians, though commenced with extremely high ideals,
had become decadent. Abbots in particular lived in great luxury
and had become as wealthy as the aristocracy. Across the previous
centuries innumerable churches throughout England had also been
extracting money from pilgrims as a result of their possession of
saint's relics. At Canterbury Cathedral the bones of the martyred
Thomas Becket were visited annually by many thousands of pilgrims.
Both in Canterbury and elsewhere the Church had become adept
at squeezing every last penny out of pilgrims anxious for a saint's
intercession.

In a political sense the age-old battle between the Church and
the Monarchy still went on. Henry's inability to obtain a divorce
from Queen Katherine was a good case in question. What was the
use of being a king if one still had to go cap in hand to a remote and
alien pope regarding the running of one's own kingdom? Some time
during the 1520s Henry had a sort of Road to Damascus experience.
Although naturally devout and at heart a good Catholic, it occurred
to him that in the eyes of God perhaps an English Catholic would
be every bit as good as a Roman one.

Henry could see a way forward that would mean he could marry
Anne Boleyn, make himself fabulously rich again and also get rid
of the interference of the Church in one fell swoop. His plan was to
dump Rome and to make himself the head of an English Church. It
must have seemed a masterstroke and would certainly be popular with
a good percentage of the aristocracy – Henry's largess when he came
into possession of the extensive Church lands would see to that.

In November 1534 Parliament passed the Act of Supremacy and
from that moment on the writing was on the wall for the abbeys and
prosperous churches of England.[23] Henry would never have taken

---

23   *Dissolution of the Monasteries*, Woodward, McIlwain, Pitkin Guides, 1993

such a bold step had he thought that the opposition from the country as a whole would be significant. He was well aware of the broad sweep of public opinion. The powerful City of York was a good example. There the townspeople regularly came to blows with the Church, in the form of St Mary's Abbey.[24] It stood within one corner of the city walls, vast and powerful, with its arrogant abbots dictating to the city fathers and generally lording it over everyone. The situation in York was not an isolated case. People all across the England, and in Wales remembered their families being exploited and even dispossessed by avaricious monks, whose powers seemed to be endless. In short, although divorcing England from Rome would cause great problems for successive monarchs, it almost certainly met with significant approval at the time. And finally, Henry knew very well that monasticism was on the wane. Some of the abbeys of England and Wales might still be very wealthy, especially in terms of the land they controlled, but as an 'ideal' they were finished. Most contained very few monks and the vast majority of the abbeys themselves had become shabby. In short, if ever an institution was ripe for dramatic change, it was the monastic houses of England and Wales.

The process of dissolving the religious houses began in 1536. It was put under the control of the ever-helpful Thomas Cromwell, who was probably the most efficient of Henry's henchmen. The procedure was the same in each case. Where abbots co-operated they were granted generous pensions, as were the monks. Once they had left the abbeys the roofs were stripped of their lead and in many cases the stone was sold off to local dealers for other buildings. When the brothers protested, they were thrown out anyway, with some being imprisoned or executed. The possessions of the abbeys came into Henry's hands, as did the hundreds of thousands of acres of land. The net income of all the abbeys of England and Wales at the time was an estimated £320,000, which represented a colossal sum during the Tudor period, though modern estimates suggest the figure was probably nearer to £400,000 or even £500,000.

---

24 *St Mary's Abbey York*, Robert William McDowall, Yorkshire Philosophical Society, 1973

In the case of the Cistercian houses, of which there were literally dozens, Henry was getting an especially good deal. As we have seen, the Cistercians were not interested in manorial holdings. They had created vast estates of large granges and even where the running of the abbey lands had passed to secular employees, the Cistercians still owned hundreds of thousands of sheep between the various houses. Henry either kept this land within the royal domains or handed large chunks of it to his followers as insurance against their compliance with his policies.

All of this happened at a very interesting time. Ever since the Black Death of two hundred years before, the established manorial system had been falling apart. What had not changed dramatically was the way land was owned by the elite but run by ordinary people. By Henry's time there were far more freeholders but farming across England and Wales was still carried out more or less as it always had been, using the three field system.

Put simply the available farmland in any village or district was divided into three units. Each of these was further divided into smallish strips and these had been historically shared out amongst the householders and the local lord. In any one year only two of the fields was farmed and the third was left fallow. Season upon season the fields rotated but by Henry's time much of the agricultural land available was 'tired' and the soil was poor. Just one of the great advantages of large numbers of sheep on much bigger fields was that they could be driven onto the land after the harvest had been gathered. There they would contentedly dispose of any stubble that remained, whilst at the same time spreading their rich manure onto the land.

In addition each community had its common land, where all villagers had been allowed to pasture their animals. This probably represented a much larger area of England and Wales than did the land available for cultivation. To the Cistercians all land was treated the same. Many of their acres were lush pasture, where sheep grazed for much of the time. If they decided to place a grange, or a part of one, under cultivation, they could be sure that the land would be in good condition and offer a high yield.

People across England had not been slow to see the advantages of the Cistercian's methods and a few of the very big landowners were already emulating them, but it wasn't an easy undertaking. It meant the destruction of whole communities and the relocations of tenants. This was a troublesome business and would only be worthwhile if the profits were significant. Once the Cistercian lands came into private ownership the truth became apparent and even those big landowners who had not inherited Cistercian lands were soon anxious to get their share of the potential profits.

Looked at from the point of view of those who controlled manors, there was really no contest between enclosed fields used to run sheep and the old three field system. Tenants were troublesome creatures. They made constant demands and for the last century or more it had been necessary to pay them for their labours. Their strips of land were unproductive – never amounting to more than subsistence farming, and the portions of land belonging to the Manor were no more productive than any of the others.

Set against this was the bounty that came from sheep. They could be tended by relatively few shepherds and would be guaranteed to offer a valuable crop of wool every year, not to mention the money that came in from mutton and skins in the case of excess animals. Even though the price of wool was not rising during the 15th and 16th centuries the prospects for sheep granges were still very attractive.

Some historians have suggested recently that the land clearances that became known as 'enclosures' came about more as a result of the rising price of wheat than the viability of sheep. This might be something of an abstraction. The planting and harvesting of crops such as wheat on a large scale was a labour-intensive operation. In any case, this still did not address the poor nature of much of the land during Tudor times. Large areas of depleted land were no more use than small strips. What made arable farming a better bet was the introduction of entirely different farming methods and the planting of crops such as clover and turnips. Although such practices were going on during the 16th century, they were not practised on any large scale and it was really the 17th and 18th centuries that brought about what has become known as the Agricultural Revolution. That was still a century or more away at the time of the Dissolution of the Monasteries.[25]

One question that must be asked is whether Britain would have arrived at the Industrial Revolution much earlier if Henry had not seized the abbey lands? This consideration runs contrary to what most British schoolchildren were and are taught. It is generally accepted that the Agricultural Revolution gave way to industrialisation and that is that – but life is not that simple.

The monasteries of England and Wales were generally in decline but this did not include all of them. Cistercians may have become lax in their religious observances but the biggest of their abbeys remained as enterprising as ever. In France the Cistercians had cornered the market in iron production, a commodity that was becoming more and more important to society as a whole. Without good, cheaply produced iron the Industrial Revolution could never have taken place at all. The Cistercians had been quick to use water power for all sorts of purposes, which included the running of very advanced forges, where water-powered hammers made light work of tasks that formerly took days. They built better carts, better roads, were experts in lead and copper smelting and also showed their enterprise by making themselves some of the best architects and builders in the world of their day.

Still, it was the production of iron, and especially cast iron, that really set the Cistercians apart. I have already mentioned the fact that archaeologists recently found something really interesting when they were digging on the land formerly owned by the Cistercian Rievaulx Abbey in North Yorkshire. What they discovered was a prototype blast furnace, which was in use at the time of the Dissolution of Rievaulx. It had previously been thought that the blast furnace was a much later invention – in fact this method of making iron wasn't considered to have been used in England until the start of the 18th century.

---

25 *Enclosure Acts: Sexuality, Property and Culture in Early Modern England*, editors Burt and Archer, Cornell University Press, 1994

A blast furnace is a device in which iron ore, limestone and charcoal are mixed in a large container and heated. Large amounts of air are then pumped through the furnace until it reaches extremely high temperatures. The result is that the heavy liquid iron sinks to the bottom of the furnace, where it can be tapped off and used, whilst the slag generally remains at the top and is removed once everything had cooled down.

The finds at Rievaulx prove that the Cistercians were using blast furnace technology at least as early as the 16th century and probably in the 15th but the Dissolution of the Monasteries stopped this technology in its tracks. Whether or not the industrialisation of Britain would have taken place earlier if the monasteries had been allowed to remain can only be conjecture. As it was, monks who understood these revolutionary processes were released into secular society, though it is unlikely they would have had sufficient funds to undertake such demanding and costly processes beyond the abbey walls.

Henry VIII could never have foreseen the consequences of his actions when he decided that a break with Rome would be best for both him and the nation he ruled. He could not know how many people within his realm would die in future generations for the sake of their faith, or how the changing religious persuasions of successive monarchs would sometimes rip the nation apart. Ultimately his actions would lead to a great civil war that would change the nature of monarchy and establish a society in which 'work' became the byword.

Sheep were an important factor in the plans of Henry VIII when he broke with Rome and took the monastery lands into his own hands. They had been an essential part of British society from earliest times and were largely responsible for the state of England when Henry VIII had come to the throne; but what they had contributed to England's rise by the 16th century was as nothing compared to what their presence would offer in the centuries that followed.

New worlds for old

Although it is almost certain that the Vikings visited parts of America in the remote past, the first European to sail across the Atlantic of whom we have absolute proof was Christopher Columbus. Columbus arrived in the Bahamas on 12 October 1492 and though he did not personally set foot on the shores of America itself on this voyage, he had proved that there was land at the far side of the Atlantic Ocean, even if it wasn't the land he had expected to find.

Christopher Columbus was born in Genoa in 1451 but although he was Italian by birth it would be in the name of Spain that his journeys to the New World would be undertaken. Columbus' father was Domenico Colombo, a wool weaver, sorter and small-time merchant as well as a local politician. His mother was Suzanna Fontanarossa, who was also from a family of spinners and weavers. Christopher chose not to follow in the family footsteps but instead embarked on a seafaring career. Little of any real note is known of his exploits in his early years at sea but it is known that by 1477 he was living in Lisbon, Portugal. By 1478 Columbus had found himself a bride. She was Felipa Perestrello e Montiz, the daughter of a fairly impoverished nobleman by the name of Bartolomeo Peristrello, who had formerly been a high ranking member of the Knights of Christ, the later Portuguese version of the Knights Templar. It is suggested by some agencies that Columbus received a number of the most useful of his Atlantic maps from the estate of his father-in-law.

In the following years Columbus gradually concocted a plan to travel to the East Indies, though by travelling west. The Indies were a great source of treasure to Western Europeans; spices in particular fetched very high prices in the markets of Italy, Portugal and Spain. There was a time when black pepper alone was worth more, ounce for ounce, than pure gold.[26]

Reaching the Indies represented a marathon overland journey but since Columbus was certain that the world was round, he was certain that the East Indies could be approached by way of a westward journey.

Despite his best efforts Columbus could not gain financial backing for his intended voyage from the King of Portugal, who was the target of his initial approaches. Instead he turned to Spain, where the co-regents Ferdinand and Isabella were much more accommodating. After lengthy negotiations Columbus was given the necessary money to mount his first expedition. This money came directly from Ferdinand and Isabella's own fortunes and was part of the profits they had been accruing from the sale of Spanish wool.

With a flotilla of just three small ships, none of which was longer than around seventy to eighty feet, Columbus set off with about one hundred men on 3 August 1492.[27] Most of what Columbus discovered on his various expeditions represents those Islands known today as the West Indies. Colonies were founded on Cuba and Hispaniola but other Spaniards soon found their way up the coast of South America and into the Gulf of Panama.

Both the Portuguese and the English looked on with avaricious eyes as the Spanish discoveries mounted. Portugal was particularly incensed, probably because it had refused to finance Columbus but also because it possessed one of the best navies in Europe at the time. England was something of a late player in terms of Atlantic exploration on any great scale and even its tentative steps were left to nationals from other parts of Europe.

---

26 *Dangerous Tastes: The Story of Spices*, Andrew Dalby, British Museum Press, 2002
27 *Christopher Columbus and the First Voyages to the New World*, Stephen C Dodge, Chelsea House Publishers, London, 1991

The first Englishman to set foot on American soil was not English at all. His name was John Cabot and he was another native of Columbus' home city of Genoa. Cabot was born in 1451, the same year as Columbus, so they were absolute contemporaries. It may indeed have been Cabot's knowledge of Columbus' voyage that had given him the idea of approaching the English Crown about a similar journey. The ever cautious and penny-pinching Henry VII of England was not so forthcoming as Ferdinand and Isabella had been and although he did support Cabot, he would only finance one ship. This was a small craft named *The Matthew*, which left Bristol in May 1497. Within a month Cabot set foot on the eastern coast of North America, most likely in Newfoundland. He returned a hero and this time King Henry was more generous. He supplied Cabot with five ships for his second expedition but apart from one craft in his flotilla that had been forced into Ireland for repairs, nothing was ever heard again of either Cabot or his ships.

It was not until the reign of Henry VII's granddaughter, Queen Elizabeth I (1533–1603), that the Americas began to become more important to the English, and then only because of a series of privately sponsored voyages that had more to do with piracy than exploration. By this time Spain had sent conquering forces into both Central and South America, bringing to an end the dominance of the civilizations that were flourishing there. The Spanish were intent on creating new colonies but their first and most important objective was gold. They systematically raped the Aztec and Inca empires of every ounce of gold upon which they could lay their hands. Most of this was melted down into Spanish currency and was then shipped back across the Atlantic in treasure ships.

England was not on good terms with the Spanish during the reign of Elizabeth – in fact Spain made one very concerted, though as it turned out disastrous attempt to invade England in 1588. The Spanish Armada, as the invasion was known, failed, but it incensed Queen Elizabeth and as far as she was concerned any Spanish treasure upon which she could lay her hands simply represented the spoils of war. Nevertheless she was careful. Instead of officially authorising attacks on the Spanish convoys, she at first simply turned a blind eye to those amongst her subjects who were willing to do so as 'privateers' – though of course she demanding a large share of the spoils from the privateers who were successful. [28]

Despite Elizabeth's protestations of innocence when faced by the rulers of countries whose ships were ravaged by the privateers it was actually in 1585, three years before the Armada, that a degree of legitimacy was granted to the English privateers. Letters of marque were issued by the high court of the Admiralty to anyone who had the intention of taking prizes from the Spanish. Upon returning to England the treasure they had captured would be split between the privateer and the state. There were many occasions on which treasure ships were captured without the privateer holding a specific letter of marque, but the Admiralty turned a blind eye to this practice just as long as the state's share was forthcoming. Thus men such as Sir Francis Drake, John Hawkins, Martin Frobisher and Sir Walter Raleigh not only made sizeable fortunes for themselves, they provided the cash that built the first true English Navy.

England might have come late to the party of carving up the spoils of a new continent but it soon began to catch up. Unfortunately the first true colony seeded by England, that of Roanoke, North Carolina, was an utter disaster. The settlement had been established by Sir Walter Raleigh in 1586 but there were severe delays in re-supplying the colonists and when new ships finally did arrive they discovered that everyone left there had disappeared without trace.

The region of the East Coast of North America known to this day as Virginia, came into existence in 1607[29]. Queen Elizabeth had died by this time, to be replaced by James I of England and VI of Scotland. Nevertheless, the new colony was named for the Queen, who because she had never married had become known as the 'Virgin Queen'. Virginia was a private venture, sponsored by a company that had been set up specifically for the purpose. Because little thought had been given to farming, the colonists nearly starved

28 *Pirates and Buccaneers*, Giles Lapouge, Hachette Illustrated, 2004
29 *American Genesis: Captain John Smith and the Founding of Virginia*, Alden T Vaughan, Oscar Handlin, Harpercollins College Division, 1995

and their numbers eventually dropped to about a third of those who had actually landed in America. However, the settlement in Virginia eventually blossomed, gaining its fame largely from the growth of tobacco. It was at this time slave-trading across the Atlantic from Africa really began, answering an ever-growing need for labour in the new colonies.

Further colonies were of a very different nature. These were funded by specific groups within society, most notable amongst these being individuals who were having religious difficulties of one sort or another at home. These settlers have became known as 'The Pilgrim Fathers' and they set up colonies that would eventually form the backbone of New England, also on North America's East Coast. The Puritans, as many of the newcomers were also known, established a colony in Massachusetts Bay and before very long the English settlements peppered the East Coast of the North American continent.

Despite the fact that most of the colonies had been formed independently, they remained under the jurisdiction of England and they represented the start of the British Empire. Although enterprising and entrepreneurial, the settlers were also quite dependent on their home country – not least for protection because so many nations from Europe were fighting over the spoils of the Americas. It didn't take long before the rulers in England began to realise that the American colonies could prove to be a good source of income. In the early years it was the efforts of individuals and companies that built the wealth of the American colonies and nowhere was this more apparent than in the case of the Cod – Wool triangle that developed in the 16th and 17th centuries.

Regina Grafe of the London School of Economics and Political Science undertook an in depth review of the developing trade, particularly to Spain, of dried codfish.[30] What she discovered is both illuminating and fascinating.

Towards the end of the 15th century dried codfish began to

---

30 *The Globalisation of Codfish and Wool,* Regina Grafe, Working Paper 71/03, Available
    for reference at http://www.lse.ac.uk/collections/economicHistory/pdf/wp7103.pdf

gain a particular importance to the Catholic countries of Western Europe and especially to Spain. Strict religious laws forbade the eating of meat on Fridays and some religious holidays. The only real alternative was fish, which itself could be a problem in the remoter inland areas of a region as big as the Iberian Peninsula. Necessity being the mother of invention, it was realised that dried fish could be kept for long periods of time and that it was possible to transport it across wide areas. Codfish was ideal for this purpose and was in ready supply. Initially, Basque fishermen roamed the Atlantic and travelled up as far as Newfoundland. The fishing fleets remained on station for long periods of time but supply ships would bring their catches back to Europe on a regular basis.

English fishermen were not slow to capitalise on such a potentially lucrative possibility and soon they too began to supply the Spanish markets. What made life easier for the English was the fact that they had good bases in Newfoundland that were necessary for the drying of fish prior to its transhipment.

By the beginning of the 17th century the supply of dried codfish became part of a wider transatlantic network of trade that would prove to be lucrative for both the English and the colonists in the Americas. This came about because of changes in the patterns of the supply of raw wool and the improving English position as suppliers of good quality finished woollen cloth.

Much of the Spanish wool that had formerly been exported to Flanders was no longer needed, mainly because of the religious wars that were being fought in the Netherlands and the destruction to the cloth trade that resulted. However, textile makers in England, and specifically in the West Country, were doing well and local sheep breeders could not supply them with all the fine quality wool they required. As a result they began to purchase Spanish wool, which was improving in quality and was readily available. Gradually, the merchants in and around Bristol created a system of imports and exports that suited their own purses and at the same time served three different markets.

There were problems with Spanish wool, most notably how it could be paid for. Gold was in short supply and in any case at an official level relations between Spain and England were not good. The West Country woollen trade needed fleeces, and the Spanish needed dried codfish. What would be more sensible than to trade one commodity against the other?

It was at this point that the origin of the codfish that was needed in Spain switched from Newfoundland to Massachusetts and Rhode Island, where all year round supplies could be guaranteed, together with a high quality of catch. The New England merchants also had their needs, most of which were forthcoming from England and in order to get the everyday and luxury goods the colonies demanded, and together with the English and Spanish merchants they established a three-way import/export business that suited everyone concerned.

Wool was shipped from Spain to England and the necessities for sustaining the colonies passed from England, and especially the West Country ports, to the East Coast of North America. Dried codfish from New England was taken to Spain, where it was used as payment for the wool.

This trade triangle also answered other problems, not least the necessity of raising large amounts of credit in order for international trade to be sustained. In effect little or no money changed hands until each of the commodities found its way to its destination. In other words revenue was raised by the selling of the wool to the West Country spinners and weavers, the normal requirements of life to the American settlers and the dried codfish to the Spanish people. Another spin-off as far as the wool trade was concerned lay in the fact that the monopoly markets owned by powerful guilds and the old woollen merchants were effectively circumnavigated. Neither were necessary in terms of the trade triangle. This also meant that smaller woollen textile producers could go it alone, buying only those quantities of wool that they needed from more local merchants, who were personally known to them. As an added bonus the local merchants were willing to allow credit terms for the raw wool, offset by the finished cloth, much of which was also destined for export.

The exchange of one set of goods for another was nothing new. It had been going on for as long as one human being needed something that he could not create or procure for himself. It was, put plain and simple, barter. What made the codfish wool triangle different was the scale upon which it was being carried out and the way it got round so many potential problems – for example the animosity that existed between England and Spain. It also clearly encouraged even more people to settle in the West Country who were already adept at the preparation of finished woollen cloth, not least amongst these being people displaced by war and religious intolerance from Flanders.

Up until the early 17th century some areas of Britain had still been exporting large quantities of wool, which found its way through Antwerp to those areas of Flanders that were still working and to the Italian markets, most specifically Florence. This came to an effective end in England in 1619 when an embargo was placed upon the export of wool from the country as a result of the needs of the home textile industry. Even prior to this date the Spanish had proved so adept at breeding sheep with good fleeces that their woollen exports outstripped those of England by eight to fourteen times.

Finished woollen cloth production was taking place in a variety of places in Europe in the 17th century but what made the situation in England, and ultimately the whole of Britain, different was the growing mercantile fleet and the fact that nowhere in Britain was very far from the sea. Just as ports in England found a way to capitalise on the codfish wool triangle, so the growing colonies in America, and their dependence on the home country, added to England's strength. Despite the fact that the country was nowhere near as rich and powerful as either Spain or France it was already sitting at the centre of a web of trading contacts that would stimulate its home industries. A different sort of population was developing. Old values, both social and religious, had been swept away by the Black Death, the Reformation and the constant need for supplies of raw wool to the cloth making process that was present in many different geographical locations.

The scene was set for a revolution so compulsive, so all-encompassing that these little islands on the Western seaboard of Europe would take on a significance in the world that would far outstrip their size. At every stage, though more as a result of serendipity than design, the right steps were being taken to provide the powder for a social and economic explosion the like of which the world had never previously known. Behind it all lay that same inoffensive little mammal that had already accompanied humanity across many thousands of years of its history. Though it did little but gaze up occasionally from its grazing on the wolds of England or the savannas of Spain, the sheep was about to change the world forever.

Defoe's epic journey

Much had changed in Britain by the beginning of the 18th century. The country had undergone a series of social disasters. These had been brought about in part by the vacillating tendencies of successive monarchs primarily because of their religious beliefs. After the Reformation of the 16th century, Henry VIII's eldest daughter, Mary Tudor, had tried to reintroduce the Roman Catholic religion to England. This trend was reversed in the reign of her sister, Queen Elizabeth I, but when the Stewart monarchs came to the throne a process of seesawing between the English Church and that of Rome began to take place.

A distrust of the King's religious affiliations and a dislike of his highhanded manner lead to a temporary end to the English monarchy in the 17th century. The merchants and middle-ranking aristocratic farmers of England were heavily represented in Parliament and they continually voted against the proposed measures of King Charles I (1600–1649). Charles believed in the divine right of kings, in other words he considered that he was responsible only to God regarding any decision he might choose to take. Parliament disagreed and the result was a bloody civil war that ravaged England, Scotland, Wales and parts of Ireland between 1642 and 1648.[31] King Charles I was eventually executed and England underwent eleven long years

---

31 *The Causes of the English Civil War*, Ann Hughes, Palgrave Macmillan, London, 1998

of rule by the Protector Oliver Cromwell. Shortly after Cromwell's death a new king, Charles II, was invited back to England but despite the fact that he tried hard to re-establish the importance of the monarch, the position had been stripped of all real power.

Charles II died childless, at least in a legitimate sense, and the throne came to his brother James, who was crowned in 1685. James II made no excuses for his Catholic persuasions and these proved to be his undoing.[32] He reigned only three years before being unceremoniously ousted from England. His place was taken by a succession of Protestant queens and kings, which lead to the foundation of a new dynasty when George, Elector of Hanover was invited to take the throne as King George I in 1714. At this time England stood as one of the more powerful of the middle ranking states of Europe but the events of the next 75 years were to propel it to heights that German George as he was called could never have envisaged.

It was in the closing years of the reign of this first King George that an Englishman by the name of Daniel Defoe decided to take a trip around Britain. The result would be one of the most fascinating books on British social history ever written.[33]

Daniel Defoe was born in London in 1660, just two years before the outbreak of the English Civil War. His father was a merchant, a member of the Butcher's Guild and a man of quite firm Protestant convictions. He wanted young Daniel to train for the Church but his son had very different ideas. Apart from being an acclaimed writer of books such as the ever-popular *Robinson Crusoe*, Daniel Defoe wrote political and religious treatise, embarked on a series of ever more unprofitable business ventures and died at seventy-one having amassed significant debts.

It was between the years 1724 and 1727 that he undertook the series of journeys that would be published as *A Tour Through the Whole Island of Great Britain*. What is so important about the work

---

32 *The Glorious Revolution of 1688*, Maurice Ashley, Hodder and Stoughton, 1966
33 *A Tour Through the Whole Island of Great Britain*, Daniel Defoe, Yale University Press, 1991

is that it gives us an excellent view of Great Britain during one of its most pivotal moments.

In the year 1707, in fact well within Defoe's own lifetime, England and Scotland officially came together, along with Wales and Ireland, to form Great Britain. This step was important because it meant that many of the difficulties that had existed between the separate kingdoms gradually faded away. It took a few more decades before many of the Scots accepted the situation but the reality of a cohesive Great Britain made the islands more of a force to be reckoned with on the European and world stage.

At the time Defoe began his journey around Britain it was teetering on a fine balance between its medieval past and its full commitment to a very different sort of future. Defoe visited all the major towns and also passed through the majority of country districts, describing what he saw in graphic detail.

Reading Defoe's account, the first major impression is just how many sheep existed across virtually the length and breadth of the islands. He estimated that on Salisbury Plain, in the south of England, there were at least 600,000 sheep, all of excellent quality and with fine fleeces. He noted a similar number in the area of Norwich, in the eastern area of England known as East Anglia. Defoe mentions significant flocks in Somerset, Devon, Wales, the Midlands, and in the North. In short he was walking through a kingdom that contained probably in excess of two to three million sheep and perhaps three or four times as many.

Defoe's Britain was certainly not industrialised in the way it would be less than a century after his journey. Areas that would become synonymous with engineering and hardware, such as Birmingham, elicit no more than a line or two from Defoe and though Sheffield is mentioned as a place famous for cutlery, it was still comparatively small in Defoe's day. Manchester was already large and growing rapidly. It was engaged heavily in the cotton trade but was fairly isolated in this regard because Defoe does not attribute cotton spinning and weaving to any of the other towns of Lancashire – rather they were involved in making either woollen or linen cloth.

Woollen textiles remained specifically important to South West England, where the towns and villages around Bristol and down towards the south coast were busy making and selling finished woollen cloth. He noted that in Gloucestershire many merchants had become incredibly rich from the wool trade. Textile manufacture was strong in and around Coventry in the Midlands, as well as in East Anglia. From Defoe's description it appears that the city of York, though still bustling and as busy as ever, was proving less important to the finished cloth trade than had once been the case. However, there is one area about which Defoe waxed lyrically and at length. This was the region in the North of England that ran eastward from the Pennines, down the valley of the River Colne and on into Airedale and what was then the township of Leeds.

It was August when Defoe visited this area, though the weather was unseasonably cold, at least on top of the Pennines, with falling snow drifting across the ill-defined track. It must have been very difficult going and Defoe makes it plain that at one stage both he and his companions were in fear of their lives. But as they walked down hill, towards the first real settlements clinging to the lower slopes of the Pennines, the sun emerged from behind the clouds and what gradually opened up before him is demonstrated by the incredulity that shines through his words as he entered the West Riding of Yorkshire.

What Defoe describes is a series of small houses, each quite separate and standing in its own small patch of land. But there were many thousands of them, stretching along roads and tracks as far as the eye could see. Almost every single house had lengths of finished cloth drying on tenters outside and the natural streams running down from the Pennines had been carefully and ingeniously channelled so that each dwelling had its own miniature river running right past its door. Everywhere was life, activity and industry, on a scale that Defoe had not encountered anywhere else on his travels – and it clearly stunned him.

'But now I must observe to you, that after having pass'd the second hill and come down into the valley again, and so still the nearer we came to Halifax, we found the houses thicker, and the villages greater in every

bottom: and not only so but the sides of the hills which were very steep every way, were spread with houses, and that very thick; for the land being divided into small enclosures, that is to say, from two acres to six or seven acres each, seldom more; every three or four pieces of land had a house belonging to it.'

Daniel Defoe was a seasoned traveller. He described in detail the congestion of London and new areas of proto-industry, like Manchester. He commented on the unceasing toil and personal peculiarities of lead miners in the Peak District of Derbyshire and the proliferation of herrings landed on the English and Scottish east coasts but it is clear to any reader that he did not expect to be confronted with what West Yorkshire had to offer.

Marvelling at the fact that the country sported so little, for example in terms of land upon which corn could be grown in such inclement weather, Defoe remained perplexed that so many people had chosen to make their homes in such desolate places, and in such unbelievable numbers. He was always asking questions and by so doing ascertained that almost everything needed for this vast number of individuals to carry out their trade on these bleak hillsides was either driven in on the hoof, for example black cattle, or else brought in by pack horse and wagons from other parts of the country.

' ... the West Riding is thus taken up, and the lands occupied by the manufacture; the consequence is plain, their corn comes up in great quantities out of Lincoln, Nottingham and the East Riding (of Yorkshire); their black cattle and horses from the North Riding (of Yorkshire); their sheep and mutton from the adjacent counties every way, their butter from the East and North Riding, their cheese out of Cheshire and Warwickshire, more black cattle also from Lancashire ...'

He also astutely hit upon another factor that set West Yorkshire apart – there were primitive but productive coal pits everywhere. Coal was not yet an important major industrial fuel, but it was needed to keep families warm in such remote and windswept areas and to heat water for the various processes that woollen cloth demanded.

Their business is the clothing trade, for the convenience of which the houses are thus scattered and spread upon the sides of the hills, as above, even from the bottom to the top; the reason is this; such has been the bounty of nature to this otherwise frightful country, that two things essential to the business, as well as to the case of the people are found here, and that in a situation which I never saw the like of in any part of England: and I believe, the like is not to be seen so contrived in any part of the world; I mean coals and running water upon the tops of the highest hills; this seems to have been directed by the wise hand of Providence for the very purpose which is now served by it, namely, the manufactures, which otherwise could not be carried on; neither indeed could one fifth part of the inhabitants be supported without them, for the land could not maintain them.'

In another section Defoe tells us:

'But now to speak of the bounty of nature again; it is to be observed, that not only on the sides, but even to the very tops, there is scarce a hill but you find, on the highest part of it, a spring of water, and a coal-pit. Having thus fire and water at every dwelling, there is no need to enquire why they dwell thus dispers'd upon the highest hills.'

Down through West Yorkshire Defoe trudged, finding broadly the same story all the way from the Pennines to the town of Leeds, which lies in the valley of the River Aire, about as far inland as it is possible to be and seventy miles from the East Coast. On the way he visited Halifax, with its huge finished cloth market – for all the world like some sort of frontier town in Defoe's day, though he noted that the woollen trade in the town had been present since at least 1480, when King Henry VII had settled people from Flanders in Halifax. He was impressed by the vitality and industry of the people and by the sheer amount of cloth passing to and fro and the sheer number of dwellings:

'I thought it was the most agreeable sight I ever saw, for the hills, as I say, rising and falling so thick,, and the vallies opening, sometimes one way, sometimes another, so that sometimes we could see two or three miles this way, sometimes as far another.......... we could see through the glades almost every way around us, yet look which way we would, high to the tops, and low to the bottoms, it was all the same; innumerable houses and tenters, and a white piece upon every tenter.'

Defoe now pointed his horse towards Leeds, some twelve miles distant. He clearly enjoyed the journey:

'From hence to Leeds, and every way to the right hand and the left, the country appears busy, diligent and even in a hurry of work, they are not scattered and dispersed as in the vicaridge of Halifax, where the houses stand one by one; but in villages, those villages large, full of houses, and those houses thronged with people, for the whole country is infinitely populous.'

Arriving in Leeds as he did from Huddersfield, which Defoe called 'Huthersfield', his journey did not bring him close to Kirkstall Abbey. The old Cistercian monastery was already a romantic ruin by his day and even if he had seen its crumbling walls it is unlikely he would have made any connection between its presence and the enterprise that existed all round him.

He found Leeds to be a very prosperous and busy place. Both in the section where he describes Leeds specifically, and in other parts of his book he makes it plain that by his day there was not a larger or more prosperous cloth market anywhere in Britain. Once again Defoe was stunned by both the number of people he encountered and the amount of provisions constantly arriving to sustain them. Of the general market in Leeds he says:

' ...and running up north almost to the Market House, where the ordinary market for provisions begins, which also is the greatest of its kind in all the north of England, except Hallifax, of which I have spoken already, nay, the people at Leeds will not allow me to except Hallifax, but say, that theirs is the greatest market, and that not the greatest plenty only, but the best of all kinds of provisions is brought hither.'

He explains in detail how on two days each week the cloth merchants and small producers brought their finished pieces to the market from miles around. The market had formerly been held on the river bridge. Trade had grown too big for that practice and by Defoe's time there was a fine cloth hall, custom built for the job. The finished pieces of woollen cloth would be laid out on trestles for the merchants to see. In absolute silence deals would be struck and despite the fact that hundreds of thousands of pounds changed hands, the whole business was finished in an hour. He says of the cloth market:

' ...which indeed is a prodigy of its kind, and is not to be equalled in the world.'

As much as a century before Defoe's time, cloth selling had already been taking place in Leeds, but on a much smaller scale. The fact that business had taken place on the river bridge just a few years earlier and that by the time of his visit it required a large building for the purpose bears testimony to how much things had changed – and how quickly.

The factors that brought about this state of affairs have only been recognised by historians fairly recently. An intensive study of trade books, both in the City of York and at ports in the north and south, demonstrate that York was losing its hold as the North's greatest textile producer. Its merchants were no longer dealing with either raw wool or finished cloth on the scale that had formerly been the case and were turning their attention in new directions. The reason seems to lie predominantly in the availability of credit. With wars on the Continent and great displacements of population in Flanders, finding the money necessary to finance the large-scale woollen production that used to take place in York had become very difficult. Smaller merchants were beginning to emerge but they preferred to deal with manufacturers who were not committed to expensive town life or to the powerful guilds. Their finance came from rich landowners in West Yorkshire, who were showing a greater tendency to speculate.

Rural woollen production was cheaper and therefore more cost-effective. Those making the woollen cloth were not subject to the taxes levied by the towns or the fees owing to the woollen guilds. The basic necessities for widespread cottage production of woollen cloth existed in the Aire Valley, that of the River Colne and in the surrounding areas. In other words there was plenty of good, soft water and abundant coal, both for domestic use and for heating water to clean the raw wool, for dye works and for fulling mills. By Defoe's day finished cloth was bypassing York and being taken straight to the London markets by the travelling merchants who bought their cloth in Halifax and especially in Leeds.

What existed from the Pennines, all the way down to Leeds was what amounted to one huge city that, by the first part of the 18th century, existed almost exclusively to serve the fantastic appetite at home and abroad for woollen cloth. As with any city, whether it congregates around a town hall and market place, or constitutes the intense ribbon development that Defoe saw, the many thousands of workers required the necessities of life.

Defoe makes it plain that there was no shortage of work available and that he saw little sign of poverty throughout the whole of West Yorkshire. Crisscrossing the area were constant strings of packhorses and heavy horse-drawn wagons, bringing in raw wool and all the commodities necessary for life. No matter how remote some of the communities of West Yorkshire were, they needed support from outside. The pack trains brought in flour for bread, pots and pans, crockery and furniture. These communities also required new spinning wheels, carding combs, teasels and everything else necessary to continue their work. Of course some of the requirements could be catered for in the locality but the fact was the West Riding had become committed, lock, stock and barrel to woollen cloth. What is more, many of the areas in question were in the uplands, where there was nothing but open, windswept moor. Even artisans in these areas had to have everything they required brought to them.

Defoe certainly did not know it but what he saw in West Yorkshire were the raw materials of a great Industrial Revolution that would make itself felt in Britain before spreading its tendrils throughout the world. Areas of the country where woollen production had fallen away were starting to service those places where it flourished, and certainly not just in West Yorkshire. One example, mentioned earlier, was Birmingham in the Midlands. Birmingham had itself once been a prosperous wool town. It's central position and close proximity to iron ore and coal had brought a gradual change, which was gaining pace by Defoe's time. Birmingham was starting its own form of specialisation. It made cooking pots, nails, buttons, chains and in fact anything that involved metal-working. Meanwhile the embryonic cutlery trade in Sheffield was also gaining pace. The presence of the necessary iron ore and the needs of rapidly growing nation were great incentives. Sheffield workers were adept in the making of 'blister steel' necessary for edged tools of all kinds.

Metalwork for building and small domestic implements were leaving the workshops of Birmingham and finding their way via established, if somewhat tortuous, trade routes, to those areas where there was industry and prosperity. Shears for clipping sheep and for trimming the nap on finished cloth, together with knives and other tools were being packed and despatched from Sheffield. In the North Midlands, where good quality clay was abundant, small, localised potteries were starting to grow. They were making flasks, crockery and, increasingly, fancy objects for a population that was starting to have some disposable income. The metal-workers bought the finished cloth and the pots made in the Midlands, whilst the cutlers of Sheffield needed the tin buttons, pins and watch chains that were produced in Birmingham. What developed was an interweaving tapestry of specialisation, all feeding common national needs.

There was nothing particularly strange about this. Medieval towns had run in a similar way. For reasons of mutual protection and convenience, trades tended to gather together. A good example is the now picturesque street in the city of York known as The Shambles. This was originally the butcher's row – shop after shop despatching animals and selling meat. From much earlier times, in fact right back to the age of the Vikings, the same city had 'Coppergate', a street that was peopled in the main by those making domestic items from copper and brass. Anyone living in York went to The Shambles for meat, and to Coppergate to buy a cheap broach for their sweetheart. There were roads peopled only by goldsmiths, silversmiths, leather workers and clothiers – all happy to be together and certain of customers who were visiting them for a specific purpose, and the same was true in every large town and city of Britain.

What Defoe saw was the same sort of tendency, but it had developed a 'regional' feel, rather than every trade being inside the same city walls. Leather manufacturers needed cows. There were plenty around Northampton, so that was where the manufacture came to be based. Making edged tools required steel, which it turn was not possible without iron. Sheffield had abundant supplies and so it specialised; to do so made sense and also offered a degree of familiarity and continuity to a community.

Nor was everything that was being created in the growing areas of specialisation intended simply for home consumption. The colonies in America and elsewhere were beginning to grow and the rapid increase in their populations brought needs they could not fulfil by their own ingenuity and hard work. With foreign colonies came the need for a significant merchant fleet, to carry people and goods back and forth across the Atlantic and elsewhere. In a world that was growing more dangerous the merchantmen needed protection, which would be supplied by a rapidly increasing Royal Navy.

Nevertheless, Defoe's Britain was still overwhelmingly rural. It is obvious from his descriptions that everyone in Britain who could practically do so was raising sheep and since Medieval times individuals had been lamenting the fact that less and less land was available across the British Isles for growing food. The picture was confused nationally because Defoe also reported that in the South of England large quantities of grain were being exported. Successful lobbying from the farming community, heavily represented in Parliament, was keeping the price of grain artificially high. This was a state of affairs that would continue until well into Victorian times. What was needed in Defoe's time were better methods of farming that would allow higher yields from less land.

Enclosure was taking place at a rapid rate.[34] The fact that so much land was being parcelled into ever greater units has been suggested as a primary reason for the growth of towns in Britain. It has been further proposed that this was the process that led to industrialisation on a grand scale. What results is a chicken and egg situation in which some experts suggest that industrialisation 'encouraged' people to move to the towns and cities, with another group maintaining that industry followed the fact that they were already there in increasing numbers.

The truth of the matter almost certainly falls somewhere between the two situations. However, the suggestion that people were forced into cities by enclosure cannot be relevant to the far-flung

34 *Commoners: Common Right, Enclosure and Social Change in England, 1700-1820,* J M Neeson, Cambridge University Press, 1996

communities of the West Riding. The cottage industry there, no matter how big it had become, took up very little of the acreage on the upland slopes, which in any case was of no real use for growing crops. Meanwhile, in the South of England, where the land was generally better, industrialisation never took place to anywhere near the same extent as it did in the North. It is abundantly clear that the main incentive for industrialisation was the introduction of machinery that took cloth production and other trades out of the cottage and into the strategically placed factory.

By the period of Defoe's Britain the ultimate industrial map of the islands was not even drawn, though there were signs of what it might eventually look like. Birmingham and Sheffield were waiting in the wings with their huge potential in iron and steel working. The Midlands were shaping up to become the pottery kings of the future. Shoemaking was developing in Northampton,. North of the border Glasgow was beginning to emerge as a commercial centre, with its own flourishing woollen textile trade. Manchester was already receiving imports of raw cotton from America and turning this into fine cloth. Liverpool and Hull were thriving ports, maintaining a regular link with countries far and near. Other great commercial centres, such as the iron and steel works of Middlesborough, the shipbuilding yards of the North East and Scotland, and huge railway towns such as Swindon in Wiltshire, all lay well into the future.

Above and beyond all was that little white animal upon whose back the entire prosperity of the British Isles ultimately depended. The sheep was still king and it seemed as though the potential for woollen cloth could never be fully exploited. The simple fact was that no matter how many regions were involved in spinning and weaving, Britain simply could not supply all the cloth it could sell. This, together with the fact that spinners could now produce more yarn than the weavers could use led to the invention of a machine that might be said to have been the most important innovation of the whole Industrial Revolution.

Inventions and evictions

In Defoe's Britain the process of spinning and weaving wool was carried on in much the same way it had always been, though by his period the number of people involved had increased tremendously. In general, supplies of raw wool were brought to cottages, where its alchemy into useable cloth was the responsibility of a whole household. It was the job of the women of the family, as well as boys and younger men, to undertake all the preparatory work, whilst the man of the house was the weaver. There were very good reasons for this. There would usually only be room in any one cottage for a single loom, which took up a significant floor area. The loom would generally be located on the first floor. In many parts of Britain old cottages can still be seen which have numerous first floor windows, the better to make use of natural light at a time when artificial light was both inadequate and expensive.

Other processes, for example spinning, needed less room, whilst scouring took place outside or in an annex built for the purpose. Dying was often undertaken in dye houses located in each district and fulling was also usually done away from the cottage by the 18th century. It is worth mentioning at this point that although finished woollen pieces enjoyed a range of different local and descriptive names by the 18th century, such as kerseys or narrows, there were basically only two types of cloth being made. Woollen cloth utilised the shorter staple of the sheep and it required intensive fulling to compress the fibres and to give the material its distinctive look and its strength. Meanwhile 'worsted', which took its name from the village in East Anglia where it was first created, employed a longer staple in its yarn. In worsted the weave of the cloth shows and because the yarn used is more resilient, it does not require fulling. This was an ideal cloth for production in East Anglia where running water to power fulling mills was not anywhere near as plentiful as on the slopes of the Pennines or in the West Country.

The raw wool was scoured, carded and spun by the family and everyone joined in as soon as they were dextrous enough to take part. The yarn was then taken upstairs where the man of the house worked his handloom. A full-grown man would normally be the tallest member of the household – probably the only family member with sufficient reach to manage the width of the cloth. He had to pass the shuttle from hand to hand through the 'shed' and though hand looms had become fairly refined by the mid 18th century, they had not changed dramatically since medieval times.

In May 1733 a young man from Bury in Lancashire applied for a patent for a machine that he described as 'A new engine or machine for opening and dressing wool'. This device has come down to us as the 'Flying Shuttle' and although it was only one of many machines that would very quickly speed up both woollen and cotton production, it could well hold the prize as being one of the most important inventions of all time – simply because it began a process in mechanisation that would lead to the world we know today.

John Kaye had been born in 1704, the son of a successful wool manufacturer in Bury, Lancashire. In Bury a sort of early industrialisation was taking place and Kaye's father owned a number of primitive textile mills. Young John showed an interest in engineering and developed skills that he applied to the trade to which he had been born. What marked the Flying Shuttle out as being of such importance was the way in which the shuttle, carrying the cross-thread known as the weft, was thrown back and forth between the warp. Instead of being passed from hand to hand, as was the case with the handloom, Kaye arranged for a device that mechanically propelled the shuttle. Since all that was required was to pull a string when the shuttle arrived at each end of the shed, the operator always had a hand free for compressing the weave that had already been produced.

It was a stroke of genius. Not only did the Flying Shuttle allow one weaver to work two and a half times as fast as on a handloom, it also meant that much wider cloth could be produced, since the width of the cloth no longer depended on the physical reach of the weaver.

What a shame that such a marvellous invention did nothing to improve the life of the man who had created it. As was to be the case across decades, workers who saw mechanisation as a threat to their livelihoods took an instant dislike to both Kaye and his loom. In 1753 they broke into his premises and destroyed a number of Flying Shuttles that were already in use. Undeterred Kaye built more, and began to work out how to supply his loom to other woollen manufacturers. They were interested, but greedy. With little to protect inventors of the period, all the local cloth producers had to do was to join forces and to refuse to pay John Kaye royalties for the use of the Flying Shuttle. The result was that the unfortunate man used up all his money fighting abortive legal battles. He eventually moved to France where history loses sight of him. It is thought that he died in poverty.

The basic reason that the cottage industry in textiles was not more productive than it was before the Flying Shuttle came along lay in a couple of specific facts. The amount of cloth being produced was directly responsive to the speed at which the weaver could work. What is more, if a family was satisfying its financial needs by turning out a couple of pieces a week, there really wasn't too much incentive for it to work any harder. The whole process was a delicate balance between spinner and weaver and the Flying Shuttle upset that balance forever.

Although the first Flying Shuttle was 'set' between each throw of the shuttle by the use of treadles, it wasn't too long before someone had the bright idea of using waterpower to run not one, but whole banks of looms. A custom built factory would be located near a reliable watercourse and a waterwheel would be used, through gearing, to power the looms. Of course only rich people could build such factories in the first place, but even those who had the wherewithal faced another problem. Many looms working together could make a great deal of cloth, but not if the weavers were sitting around for much of the time waiting for yarn. By the middle of the 18th century Lancashire alone had 50,000 people solely committed to spinning, and yet still there wasn't enough yarn being produced. The way was open for another machine, this time one that could deal with the problem of spinning quickly.

Enter a little known man by the name of Thomas Highs. His real name was probably Hays, which was misspelled by the registrar at the time of his birth in 1718. Thomas Highs came from Leigh in Lancashire and it appears that he was an engineer, rather than a woollen worker. He is thought to have been a 'reed maker'. A 'reed' was the comb-like metal strip through which the threads of the warp passed on the loom. It was the device that kept the threads apart and which allowed the weaver to compress the weft threads up against the already woven cloth.

One day, the son of a friend, who called at his house after spending a whole day in a fruitless search for yarn so that his father could continue weaving, alerted Highs to the lack of yarn being produced. Highs teamed up with a neighbour, a poor and illiterate clockmaker by the name of John Kay (not to be confused with John Kaye, who invented the Flying Shuttle). Together they worked on, and eventually refined, a machine that was capable of spinning several different threads at the same time. John Kay seems to have lost interest in the device when its intricacies proved to be frustrating, but Highs persevered.

It was around this time that Highs turned for assistance to another neighbour, a man by the name of James Hargreaves. Hargreaves had been born in Blackburn and was both a carpenter and a woollen weaver. The two met in the village of Stanhill and co-operated on the machine that Highs had already christened the 'Spinning Jenny'. Nobody knows for sure why it was called a Jenny. It could have been named after Highs' wife, Jane, but more likely the name stemmed from the apparent 'magic' of the machine's operation. In the North of England a 'Jenny' was the name given to a witch and this might have seemed appropriate for such a wondrous and unfathomable device.

Eventually Highs and Hargreaves went their separate ways, each taking the idea for the Jenny with them and developing it in slightly different ways. The Jenny used eight spindles onto which the thread was spun via a sort of wooden vice that kept it taut. It needed only the turn of one wheel to make all eight spindles work, effectively revolutionising the whole spinning process. Both Highs and Hargreaves at first envisaged a machine that might be suitable for home production but like the Flying Shuttle the Spinning Jenny lent itself ideally to mechanisation.

The Spinning Jenny did have one problem, particularly in Lancashire where it was used for cotton rather than wool. It was not capable of spinning warp threads, merely those for the weft. Up until this time warp threads in the cotton weaving trade had usually been made from linen, a yarn made from the flax plant. It had not been possible to create sufficiently strong warp threads from cotton and the first Spinning Jenny did not remedy the problem. Hargreaves nevertheless continued work on the Jenny, whilst Highs went on to create a better machine that he called 'The Water Frame'. The Water Frame used two sets of rollers to grip the threads. Such was the gearing of the machine that one set of rollers moved at five-times the speed of the other set. By way of a device known as a 'bobbin and flyer' and the rollers, a much better and tighter cotton thread was achieved and this was ideal for the warp yarn.

At this point a man who was something of a rogue enters the story. He was Richard Arkwright, who was from Bolton in Lancashire. Arkwright was a barber and a maker of wigs but he was a man who was always on the lookout for a good idea. Arkwright seems to have befriended Kay, who was no longer associated with Highs, though Kay was aware of the intricacies of both the Jenny and the Water Frame. Taking advantage of Kay, Arkwright managed to get hold of the working principles of the Water Frame. He persuaded Kay to make a model of the device and used it to procure funding from a financier in Preston, passing the machine off as his own.

Arkwright then employed Kay, together with another engineer, to make a full-sized version of the Water Frame, which turned out to be more or less exactly the same device perfected by Highs. Arkwright's greed and duplicity nearly rebounded on him. In 1781 he lost the patents for the Water Frame and in 1785 he went to court to try and regain them. It was at this time that Highs reappeared, accusing Arkwright of stealing his invention. It did him no good because although Arkwright's patents were set aside, he went on to become colossally rich, whilst Highs disappeared into obscurity.

The spinning process was refined by Samuel Crompton, who was born in 1753, in Bolton, Lancashire. In 1775 he created a device that became known as a 'Spinning Mule' because it was a hybrid between the Jenny and the Water Frame. Crompton was a good inventor but a bad businessman and he ended up being cheated out of his rights to the Mule. Uncharacteristically, Parliament felt sorry for him and thanks to the politician Robert Peel, Crompton was awarded £5,000 from the Government's purse. With his usual business acumen Samuel Crompton promptly invested the money into a cotton factory, but despite a market that was crying out for cotton cloth, he contrived to go bankrupt.

Cotton is derived from the seed heads of the cotton plant. The plant is a member of the genus Gossypium of the family Malvacaea and is part of a group of plants commonly known as Mallow. Cotton was first used to make fabric as early as 3,500 BC in India and 3,000 BC in Peru. Textiles made from the cotton plant are light in weight and ideal for garments worn in warm climates. Early colonists in the US discovered that the climate there, more especially in the southern states, was ideal for the cultivation of cotton. The only problem was that cotton production was a very labour-intensive business. It wasn't until the introduction of slavery into the infant US that there were sufficient workers to manage a sizeable crop. Even by the 17th century relatively small amounts of raw cotton were finding their way to England, where they were often mixed with linen to make a cloth that was usually known as 'Fustian'.

Some care is necessary with regard to the word cotton as used in documentation, even up until the early 18th century. This is because although the word became attached to the plant that now carries the name, it existed previously as a term that described the 'finish' of a cloth – and especially a woollen cloth. Where a deliberate nap or furry surface was required, this was often referred to as 'cottoned wool'. Strangely enough, even by as late as 1822, woollen clothes provided for slaves in the US were still being called 'cottons'. It is just possible that the word derives from a source that originally meant 'coating' and therefore applied to woollen fabric that was specifically designed for the making of coats. Some historians have been misled regarding just how early in English history significant amounts of the fabric we now call cotton was actually being produced locally, though there is no doubt that cotton textile production was significant in and around Manchester by the early 18th century.

Cotton fabric was not popular with people in Britain *en masse* until late in the 19th century because it remained quite expensive and was impractical for most ordinary purposes in the cool climate of the British Isles. Nevertheless, as it became cheaper to produce, and when the disposable income of ordinary people began to rise, cotton fabric, considered distinctly luxurious, fell within the reach and the desirability of almost everyone.

The production of cotton fabric in England was attractive because there was always a significant market for it amongst the 'well to do'. Originally, it had been imported in significant quantities from India but home production both reduced the price of the finished cloth and acted as a significant spur to export.

Of all of the inventors of the first machines that would revolutionise fabric production, the only one who truly gained as a result of his efforts was the individual who had the least right to do so. Richard Arkwright carries the accolade as being the father of the factory system of production. Arkwright, with Kay still in tow, went to live in Preston, where he developed his machine and opened a small spinning mill. His enterprise soon attracted the attention of the disgruntled weavers, who threatened to smash his machines. As a result he moved again, this time to Nottingham, where the 'Luddites' as those breaking up machines had become known, were not operating. Together with new business partners,

John Smalley and David Thornley, Arkwright opened a mill in the Hockley district of the city, close to where James Hargreaves also had a factory that was using his version of the Spinning Jenny.

The mill was moderately successful but limited because it was powered by horses turning a treadmill. Wishing to streamline the process even more, Arkwright now turned to two businessmen, Jebediah Strutt and Samuel Need, and together they created a custom-built factory at Cromford in Derbyshire, this time run by powerful waterwheels. All that held Arkwright back after his move to Derbyshire was the fact that a sizeable import tax existed on raw cotton. This had come about as a result of pressure from the wool lobby, which wanted to protect its own interests. In 1774 the tax was removed and it wasn't long before Richard Arkwright began to grow extremely rich.

With the new machines now available for both cotton and woollen cloth production, those with money, particularly in the North of England, clamoured to build mills of the sort that Arkwright had pioneered. The presence of such factories quite soon began to change the whole structure of cloth production and on the way it also altered the lives of many thousands of people.

Because machines such as the Spinning Jenny and the Water Frame were so efficient, they could turn out finished pieces in a fraction of the time that was possible with home production. This meant that the resulting cloth could be sold cheaper, effectively driving the cottagers out of the market. Most of the huge proliferation of people Defoe had seen working away in their homes in the Colne and Aire Valleys would eventually be forced, by sheer economics, to move to places where the new mills existed, there to seek employment. The same was true on the other side of the Pennines in Lancashire, where cotton production rapidly spread out from Manchester. The only reason cotton did not also become established in Yorkshire had more to do with the climate than any economic factor. The atmosphere on the west side of the Pennines is damper than on the eastern slopes. This suited the needs of cotton spinning, which was less successful in a dry atmosphere.

Those areas of Britain that did not enjoy fast flowing streams capable of turning water wheels were immediately at a great disadvantage. There was nothing new about waterpower, which had been used for purposes such as grinding corn and running the bellows for forges for many centuries. It had been particularly pioneered by the monastic orders, such as the Cistercians, but even they had not invented the waterwheel, which was mentioned in England as early as the Doomsday Book in 1087.

Even the textile trade had been using waterpower for a considerable period. Waterwheels had been used for some time before the 18th century to drive great hammers in the fulling mills. Now harnessed to spinning and weaving, waterwheels began to break down the very structure of life in the cloth producing areas. Not only were workers more or less forced to relocate to areas where mills were being established, other individuals had to rethink their own strategies.

Textile production, both in terms of wool and also cotton, had relied on the 'piece system'. Local merchants, usually businessmen with only a limited amount of capital, would buy raw wool, either locally or from import merchants. They would take this to people living in and around their locality, where it would be processed into finished cloth. The merchant would return at a predetermined time to collect the cloth, at which time he would pay the family in question for its work. He would then collect together the finished pieces from a number of families and take these off to a local market, for example the one at Leeds, and sell the cloth on into the home or export markets. His profit came from the price he obtained for the finished cloth, which was greater than the money he had laid out on the raw wool and its transformation.

There wasn't much scope in this system for the merchant to become either more efficient or richer. His efficiency and his income was governed by the distance he could travel in any given week and even if he took on hired help, this would not boost his earnings to any great extent. Factories created economy of scale and they eventually forced the travelling piece merchants out of the market altogether. Those owning the mills could secure better prices on huge amounts of raw wool or cotton. Their overheads, although great in contrast to those of the cottager, were much less per unit produced and wasted labour was cut out of the system. For example, one woman, or even a girl, could attend to a machine or a bank of machines, that could spin yarn at perhaps a hundred times the rate of the same girl operating a traditional spinning wheel.

Richard Arkwright had shown the way forward, but it was certainly at the expense of the quality of lives of those who came to work for him. There were no rules during the 18th century regarding the employment of children and wherever possible Arkwright used child labour, mainly because it was so cheap. It also suited his purposes to keep his mill working as long as possible in any given day – after all, the river kept running day and night. This meant very long hours for the workers, especially in summer when there was plenty of daylight, which like the waterpower was essentially free.

Another problem was housing. Before the advent of steam power, mills had to be placed where there was sufficient water to turn the millwheels. Some mill owners who could afford to do so built housing close by, to ensure that their workers were available and this brought about a situation in which the workers were inextricably tied to their employment. Formerly the lives of so many thousands of people across Britain had responded to the clock of nature. They rose when it was light and worked steadily through the day, stopping for meals when they wished and also able to give some time to other tasks in and around their homes. With the advent of the mill they became wage slaves, whose lives were governed by a time clock and a factory whistle.

At the same time as thousands of little cottages on the slopes of the Pennines began to fall into crumbling heaps of stone, people far away from the new woollen production mills themselves were also suffering as a result of the mechanisation. Greater production meant more sales, both within Britain but especially to the export trade. However, increased volume also meant that the desire for good quality wool became ever greater. Britain, a country that had always been a net exporter of raw wool now kept practically all of its fleeces for home production and also began to import wool on a much larger scale.

Supplies of the best quality wool were limited and importation was expensive. Even the cost of home produced wool began to rise as the laws of supply and demand kicked in. There was greater incentive than ever for farmers, and especially owners of large areas of suitable land, to go into sheep rearing. Taken together with political events that were unfolding in Britain at the same time as mechanisation and waterpower was making textile mills viable, hundreds of thousands of people were about to lose their homes and in many cases even the nation of their birth.

The Scots had been a thorn in the side of England for many centuries. Although the Act of Union of 1707 had created Great Britain, this was not a state of affairs that suited everyone north of the border. A significant number of Scots still had an allegiance to the old Stuart kings, who were languishing in France, awaiting any opportunity to return. Uprisings had taken place in 1689, 1705, 1715 and 1719, as the displaced Scottish monarchs had sought to re-establish their thrones. The adoption of the German George I as king of Great Britain in 1714 had done nothing to secure the loyalty of many Scots and although the uprisings of 1715 and 1719 were put down with great aggression, the final showdown would not come until 1745.

James Stuart, known to many Scots as James VIII sent his son, Charles Stuart, from France to Scotland in July 1745. There he gathered a large army, composed mainly of Highland Scots and he began to march south into England. Surprisingly the Jacobites, as they were called, met with little resistance, partly because the bulk of the English army was either on the Continent or in Ireland at the time. The rebel army got as far south as Derby before its leaders were panicked by reports of a large English army coming their way. The rumours were false and had the Highlanders continued south, they could probably have taken London. Instead they retraced their steps northward and set the seal on their own annihilation.

The decisive battle came in April 1746 on a windswept moor near Inverness. The place was called Culloden and amidst its wind-blasted vegetation the hopes of Scotland would seep into the mud with the blood of its sons. When the battle was over, the English were victorious and the Highland army was utterly routed. By now, George II occupied the British throne. Neither he nor the ruling forces in the South were in any mood to leave the Scottish Highlands in a position that would allow the clans to rise again. A conscious decision was taken to destroy Highland life forever.

After the Battle of Culloden the English army, which to be fair also contained a large number of Lowland Scots, swept through Northern Scotland, rooting out Jacobite sympathisers. Clans were broken up and many Scottish lords, or lairds as they were known, were either executed or banished. Their lands were given to supporters of the Hanoverian Crown in London. These new lairds were frequently Lowlanders, who had no desire to remain on their domains in the harsh Scottish weather, miles away from what they considered civilized society. Many of them actively chose lives far away from Scotland, close to the cosy London Court of which they were an increasingly important part.

The huge Highland areas they had inherited were generally unproductive. The best they could sport were small, inefficient farms, generally run by individual families at a subsistence level. Rents from these properties were minimal and yet there were hundreds of thousands of acres of land that were ideal for the rearing of hardy northern sheep. What would be better than to get rid of future political problems and to rid the Highlands of tenants who were clearly more trouble then they were worth? What followed has become known as the Highland Clearances.

All across the Highlands whole communities were relocated, sometimes forcefully, to other areas, often closer to the coast. Lives that had depended for countless centuries on small family farms, were thrown into chaos. All too often the result was starvation and the situation could only be remedied by mass emigration. Literally thousands of Scots shipped out to Canada or the US, or at the very least moved south to the developing industrial areas of Lowland Scotland and England. The same was generally true in Ireland, where troublesome tenants were also 'encouraged' to leave the shores of their own ancestral lands and to start a new life far away.

There is no doubt that the policy of clearance and enclosure was a tragedy for the British Isles, at least as far as the lives of the people in question was concerned but in the fullness of time the presence of all these newcomers in North America would help immeasurably in the creation of new nation states. The land seized to rear more sheep in Scotland and Ireland boosted the numbers of settlers in both Canada and the US to such an extent that both nations began to develop more quickly as a result. It is therefore a fact that the unsuspecting sheep was primarily responsible for giving the colonies the labour force they so badly needed. However, in the case of the US the situation went even further because sheep also contributed significantly to its eventual independence.

The sheep goes west

Though there were no domestic sheep in either North or South America prior to the arrival of Europeans, North America does have a wild sheep of its own. This is called the Bighorn Sheep and its Latin name is *Ovis Canadensis*. The Bighorn is a majestic creature that still lives in the wild in two very different settings. The Mountain Bighorn is to be found in the Rocky Mountains, from Southern Canada down to Colorado, whilst the Desert Bighorn is specifically adapted to more arid conditions and lives in the Sierra Nevada Mountains of California and in South Mexico. The species is under threat and has disappeared altogether from some of its historical ranges but extensive efforts are underway to protect remaining Bighorns and to breed new sheep to release into the wild.

The Bighorn sheep is a muscular animal, ranging from grey to dark brown in colour and the breed is particularly distinguished by the fact that the horns of the older males begin to curl around. Although this animal has been extensively hunted by man for thousands of years, it has never been domesticated and so retains a coat that is more hair than wool. One of the problems the Bighorn has faced, apart from being extensively hunted, is that its natural grazing has been taken for domestic animals and especially the European sheep.

When the first Spanish expeditions arrived in Central and South America, the Conquistadors as they were known, brought with them their own form of hardy Spanish sheep, which were called 'Churros'. The Churros is typical of the sort of sheep that were bred in Spain prior to the creation of the Merino, which is a less hardy animal but one that carries wool of an excellent quality. The Merino did exist by the 16th century and ultimately it too was brought to the US, Central and South America. However, the first expeditions mounted by the Spanish were intended as visits of conquest. The armies of men such as Francisco Pizarro and Herman Cortes, were moving quickly. They were soldiers, not farmers, and they needed animals that could forage for themselves and yet move significant distances along with the troops. The tough little Churros were ideal. Churros breed readily and can supply both mutton and fairly good wool.

The arrival of the Churros, like that of the Spanish themselves, would have a tremendous effect on both South and Central America. But although the domestic sheep was unknown in the Americas until the 16th century it did have an important counterpart. The culture encountered by the Spanish in South America was that of the Inca.[35] The Incas controlled a huge empire that spread down the West Coast of South America, from Ecuador in the north, down through modern Peru and Bolivia, down into parts of Argentina. Inca society was extremely organised, though apart from a little gold working, it had remained a Stone-Age culture up until the Spanish conquest.[36] Not that the Inca were in any way backward. On the contrary they had fantastic trading networks, were expert farmers and were particularly adept at spinning and weaving.

Like peoples further north, in Central America, the Inca were well aware of the existence of cotton, which they readily used in their textiles. Cotton, and other plant fibres were fine for clothes worn at low altitudes or in those regions closer to the equator, but much of the Inca's vast land lay on the mountain slopes of the Andes. At these high altitudes the temperatures can be extremely low and textiles such as cotton cannot supply sufficient warmth. Fortunately

35   *Realm of the Incas*, Max Milligan, Idlewild, 2003
36   *The Incas (Peoples of America S.)* Terence N D'Altroy, Blackwell Publishing, 2003

for the Inca they had their own version of the sheep, which though a very different sort of animal, served much the same function. The Inca kept large herds of both Llamas and Alpacas, two creatures that are members of the camel family. The Llama supplies a fairly coarse form of wool, ideal for hard-wearing outer garments, whilst the Alpaca had been selectively bred to produce a much softer wool, from which luxuriant fabrics were made by the more than competent Inca weavers.

Llamas and Alpacas are closely related to both Bactrian and Dromedary camels, though they are considerably smaller in size and don't have the camel's distinctive humps. They are to be found in a range of colours and were herded on a huge scale by the Inca. The finest of the wool was reserved for the Inca royalty and aristocracy and those scraps of genuine Inca textiles that do exist show just how dextrous and artistic Inca weavers could be.

The Inca civilization was not a long-lasting phenomenon, in fact it did not endure for much more than a century. It was composed of a number of disparate people, welded together, partly by coercion and conquest but also by the need to trade across vast areas. The Inca certainly used the herding skills of the Andean shepherds but the practice had already existed for centuries before the rise of the Inca Empire. The Llama and the Alpaca were, to the people of the region, exactly what the sheep was to people all over Europe and Asia. In addition to be being prized for its hair, and in the case of the Llama as a light draft animal and the meat of both animals was also eaten.

Further north, in Mexico, the Spaniards found themselves facing the empire of the Aztecs. This was a civilization like no other and had developed a religious base that revolved around human sacrifice on a colossal scale. Nevertheless the Aztecs were capable farmers and animal breeders; they enjoyed diverse food sources and created fine textiles. Mexico enjoys a very hot climate, so there was never a need for wool of any sort. Clothes, which for men especially often represented little more than a loincloth, were usually made of cotton or maguey fibres, though it is possible that some Llama or Alpaca wool was imported from further south. If so, this would have been highly prized by the ruling elite amongst the Aztecs and would certainly have served a ceremonial rather than a practical purpose.

It did not take the Spaniards long to conquer vast areas of land in Southern and Central America and up into Mexico. Almost immediately sheep breeding was taken on board by local peoples, who soon became adept at spinning and weaving wool, creating the same extraordinarily detailed patterns that they had developed for other textiles, across many centuries. Sheep raising and textile production became important component parts of the economies of lands settled by the Spanish, in both Central and South America. To many of the native peoples of these regions, and to those of the southern US, the sheep soon became an essential and revered part of life.

It was the Spanish churros that formed the bulk of sheep herds during the start of the colonial period across much of America and when settlers from Britain started to build colonies down the Eastern seaboard of North America, and in particular in the southern states, they acquired churros, which were already well adapted to local conditions.

Once colonization became the norm, European farmers who came to control land in the Americas wanted to create the same sort of circumstances they had known in their ancestral lands. Sheep were almost immediately an essential part of life, especially in New England and other settlements in the East. There the weather can be bitter in winter and woollen clothes were crucial to survival. Sheep thrived in these areas and the problem faced by the colonists was not one of raising sheep, but rather of the form of control exercised from Britain.

The development of the British colonies in North America might have been very different, were it not for the prevailing circumstances in the period during which they were beginning to grow and prosper. At first the British were not willing to allow many sheep to be taken to the colonies, probably because they recognised the tremendous potential for sheep rearing in such large and verdant surroundings. In order to understand why, we need to look at what was happening in Britain and the world at the time.

There was fierce competition in North America between the British and the Dutch, who were also establishing colonies and outposts. As an example, New York was originally named New Amsterdam and did not come into British hands until 1664. Anxious to protect its interests on the American continent, Britain continually passed laws that were in its own interests, but which became more of a thorn in the side of the colonists as time passed.

By the end of the 17th century the woollen textile industry in Britain was eclipsing every other trade and the British were keen to retain their monopoly. Had the British authorities realised what would happen in the latter part of the following century, they may have actually encouraged Americans to raise vast numbers of sheep, in which case the development of the American colonies might have been very different. Those ruling Britain could not know that by the start of the 19th century they would be starved of foreign wool because of their opposition to the French and particularly to Napoleon. As it was the British Parliament could see no reason to allow the American colonies to develop a sheep breeding and woollen textile base, which might detract from Britain's own success and would limit the number of imports the Americans needed.

Undeterred, the first European American farmers obtained sheep from Spanish and Dutch sources and the local manufacture of woollen textiles began to gain ground. At first this simply represented the same sort of cottage industry that had been taking place in Britain for so long. The first European Americans were not so much concerned with selling their finished textiles, except in a very local sense. What really motivated them was having clothes to wear!

The British watched the developing situation from a very early stage. About fifty years after the Pilgrim Fathers had landed at Plymouth Rock, the settlers had purchased forty British sheep from the Dutch on Manhattan Island and the London Company had also imported sheep as early as 1609. These sheep, together with those acquired from the Spanish, formed the nucleus of rapidly increasing flocks and ultimately led to a surplus of wool that the colonists could trade for goods they needed. So jealous of its own trade was Britain that it passed a local law that meant anyone in the colonies trading in wool could have a hand cut off.

The Wool Act of 1699 represented an important first step in building the resentment amongst the colonists that would eventually lead to the Revolution and the break with Britain. The Government in Britain could see the potential in American wool and developed a protectionist policy designed on the one hand to preserve the British textile trade, whilst at the same time keeping the colonists inextricably tied to the old country. The Wool Act stated that American colonists could not ship any raw wool, woollen yarn or finished woollen textiles to any country whatsoever.

Most historians these days concentrate on later British Acts of Parliament that came on the eve of the general uprising in the American colonies. What they sometimes fail to point out is that anger had been simmering in the British colonies for many decades before action was taken. A part of this animosity was fostered by such ridiculous notions as the Wool Act, a measure that stopped commercial sheep rearing in the infant US in its tracks.

The powerful merchants of Boston eventually took a stand. In May 1763 they organised a boycott of luxury goods imported from Britain, which angered the British government and spurred it into taking ever more draconian actions against the colonists. As far as the wool trade was concerned, what made matters worse for the Americans was a Pennsylvania engineer by the name of James Davenport had created a machine that could both card and spin wool successfully, This was the first real sign of industrialisation within North America but no matter how adept the Americans became in the wool trade, British policies effectively barred them from the textile markets across the world.

By 1775, with a new stamp duty and a ridiculous tax levied by the British on tea, the colonists had reached the end of their patience. What followed was a protracted war of independence that resulted in the British being ousted from its former colonies in America. The war lasted eight long years, which were a time of great hardship for the colonists, who had been forced to rely heavily on imports from Britain, even though their potential for self-sufficiency was tremendous. Such was the shortage of warm clothing during the struggle that not only did the revolutionary government encourage sheep rearing and home textile production, it 'ordered' every family to keep sheep and to produce cloth.

Once the US became a reality, it began to concentrate on building up its own exports. Fortunately the animosity between the US and Britain did not last too long, mainly because Britain needed the raw materials that the US could supply, chief amongst which were large amounts of cotton. The bans on American wool enforced by Britain for so long actually prevented sheep rearing in the US from becoming what it eventually would in Australia and New Zealand because by the time Britain and America were trading again, cotton was all the rage. Wool still predominated in Britain but during much of the 18th century supplies of raw wool were readily available. Nevertheless, with more and more settlers arriving all the time, the original states began to send out explorers to the West. The trailblazers were quickly followed by settlers, some of whom found the extensive grasslands of the Midwest ideal for sheep rearing.

During much of the 19th century and into the 20th there was fierce competition across large swathes of North America between cattle breeders, sheep breeders and farmers. In the lawless West and down into Texas these struggles often led to violence, intimidation and ultimately legal wrangles once the region had been tamed. Generally speaking the cattle ranchers were more successful and although the US became a sizeable breeder of sheep circumstances conspired to prevent it from becoming the really huge player in both raw wool and finished woollen cloth that it might have been.

There are several reasons for this but the most important lay in the fact that Australia was discovered and colonies were created there immediately before the American War of Independence. When the Industrial Revolution really started to gain ground in Britain it was towards Australia that Britain turned its attention in terms of sheep breeding. Almost from the word go Australia could raise sheep more cheaply than was possible in the US. Part of the reason for this lay in the fact that labour in Australia was cheap, being composed largely of convicts transported there from Britain. This is not to suggest that sheep rearing in the US has been unimportant to the nation's economy. Nevertheless, at the last count there were around 6,000,000 sheep in the US and although this is a significant number it is less than 1% of the total world sheep population.

By the time Britain's textile industry was being starved by the Napoleonic Wars, at the beginning of the 19th century, the US was already an independent entity. As its population grew and new territories were opened to Europeans, its true potential became obvious. But what America could not manage was to catch up with cheap woollen textile manufacture in the face of what was taking place in Britain. Neither could it compete with the sheep-rearing potential of Australia and New Zealand.

Nevertheless the use of wool in the US is still significant. In addition to raw wool from its own flocks the US presently imports $17.5 million of wool from Australia on an annual basis. As a proportion of the $3.9 billion in total wool exports this is small but at the same time the US does also export wool, in fact about 1% of total world raw wool exports.

The true importance of the sheep to the US cannot really be judged in terms of how important the animal has been to US development in a direct sense. Rather it is the overall significance of the sheep to those events in history that ultimately led to the formation of the United States of America that is significant. It was Britain's growth that saw the country developing a sizeable merchant and fighting fleet. This allowed Britain to fight off the competing interests of the Spanish, Portuguese and Dutch on the North American continent. The gradual growth of Britain had been, from earliest times, dependent on Britain's vast herds of sheep and the wool they produced. Without them Britain would almost certainly have proved less successful and may have been nothing more than a sleepy European backwater.

Britain was not alone in having been radically altered by the presence of the sheep. In great measure the European trade in wool and textiles had lead to the Renaissance and then to religious reformation. In turn this resulted in the religious wars that ravaged some of the most productive woollen textile centres of Europe.

Britain reaped the reward and became by far the greatest net producer of woollen textiles. Religious upheavals and the needs of an ever greater sheep population led to mass migrations from Britain and these people proved crucial in the development of the US. People from the Celtic fringes, and especially Scotland, were amongst the most important and productive settlers in both the US and Canada. They had been forced to leave their own ancestral lands but their hard work and eventual success helped to make North America into the industrial and economic giant it is today. How very different the world might have looked without the unknowing but insistent influence of the humble sheep!

The continent in the south

On Sunday 27 October 1728 James Cook took his first tentative breath in the small village of Marton, close to modern Middlesborough, in Yorkshire. James was the son of another James - a poor day labourer who would undertake dry-stone walling, ploughing, ditching or any other job that would earn a modest sum from the honest sweat of his brow. James junior was baptised a week later at the local parish church of St Oswald.[37]

There was no money to spare in the Cook household and legend has it that almost as soon as young James was old enough to take on the responsibility he was tending to whatever task he could procure from the local farmers. There is a persistent rumour that part of his duties involved tending the flocks of hardy northern sheep that speckled the fields near his home.

By 1736 James senior had secured a much better position, as the 'hind' or foreman on the manor farm of Thomas Skottowe, Lord of the Manor of Great Ayton, not far from where James had been born. With a little more money to spare James could attend Postgate School, in his local village, though this was only part time and he still worked on the farm whenever he could. Thomas Skottowe was a good employer to James Cook senior and it was he who introduced young James to one William Sanderson, a shopkeeper from Staithes, North Yorkshire. As a result James left home in 1745 and travelled

37 *Journals of Captain Cook, Prepared by J C Beaglehole*, Penguin Classics, 1999

the twenty miles or so to the little fishing village, which lies a few miles north of Whitby. [38]

The story goes that James was not settled in the grocers and haberdashers shop where he had gone to learn a trade and that he spent a good deal of his spare time looking out to sea, or else in the cramped little harbour, learning what he could about boats from the fishing cobbles that bobbed about on the tide. He seems to have been popular with his employer, who realising the lad's longing for adventure introduced him to John and Henry Walker, who lived and worked in Whitby where they ran several coal ships that sailed along the North Sea coast from Newcastle down to London, loaded with fuel for the hearths of the capital. Exactly what position James held in the business of the Walkers is not known but it wasn't long before the records of the company show him aboard ship and learning how to be a seaman.

In addition to plying the North Sea, which represents some of the most treacherous waters in the world, both before and after his apprenticeship James Cook had travelled up into the Baltic, across to the Continent and to Newfoundland. But it was on one of his visits to London that he met and married Elizabeth Batts, the daughter of an associate of the Walkers.

In 1755 James Cook surprised all his relatives and friends by leaving his secure berth on *The Friendship* and enlisted in the Royal Navy as an able seaman. He was first posted to a ship called HMS *Eagle* and within a couple of months his experience was recognised and he was made Master's Mate. Cook saw action many times in the years that followed. Britain was invariably at war during this period and there was no shortage of excitement for the brave and resourceful young man that James seems to have been.

Cook took a particular delight in exploration and undertook journeys around the coast of North America and into the Great Lakes. There he compiled charts and navigated unknown passages, all the time gaining in the esteem of his superiors and the Navy generally and eventually gaining the rank of captain.

---

38   *Captain James Cook*, Richard Hough, Coronet Books, 2003

The piece of luck that led to the voyage that would put Cook into the history books was the calculation that a transit of Venus would take place in 1769. This meant that Venus would pass across the face of the sun. A Venus transit was an event of supreme importance to astronomers but it would be best seen from the Pacific Ocean. Cook was chosen to captain the expedition and was given a converted coal ship, which was renamed *Endeavour*.[39] On 30 July 1768 Cook's ship weighed anchor in London and set off on one of the most exciting voyages of the 18th century.

In addition to his instructions to find a suitable location from which to observe the Transit of Venus, Cook also carried secret orders, concerning a possible continent in the southern hemisphere. The Dutch were already convinced of the existence of the place they called Nova Hollandia (New Holland) but they thought it was an extension of New Guinea, part of which had been sighted and mapped as early as 1627. It was a Dutch captain, Abel Tasman, who would confirm what was already suspected. In his first voyage, commenced in 1642, Tasman sailed out into the Pacific from Batayia and visited Fiji and Tonga. Doubling back to the south west he visited both the North and South Islands of New Zealand and then happened upon Tasmania, the large island to the south of Australia. It was originally named van Dieman's Land, after Tasman's employer, but eventually it was renamed after the first European to visit its shores.[40]

On his second voyage, in 1644, Abel Tasman sailed along much of the north coast of Australia. He went ashore in several places but does not seem to have claimed the land for the Dutch and nor did he consider its potential for colonization. As no financial gain was forthcoming the Dutch East India Company, for whom Tasman was ultimately working, considered his trips to be of little value.

How much of this was known to the Royal Navy remains a mystery, though it was certainly aware of Tasman's journey to New

---

39 *"Endeavour": The Story of Captain Cook's First Great Epic Voyage*, Peter Aughton, Phoenix, 2003
40 *Voyages of Abel Janzoon Tasman*, Andrew Sharp, Oxford University Press, 1968

Zealand. The British Navy seems to have been slightly less sure about the massive landmass to the west of New Zealand and Cook's secret orders stated:

'Whereas the making Discoverys of Countries hitherto unknown, and the Attaining of Knowledge of distant Parts which though formerly discover'd have yet been but imperfectly explored, will redound greatly to the Honour of this Nation as a Maritime Power, as well as to the Dignity of the Crown of Great Britain, and may trend [sic] greatly to the advancement of the Trade and Navigation thereof; and Whereas there is reason to imagine that a Continent or Land of great extent, may be found to the Southward of the Tract lately made by Captain Wallis in His Majesty's Ship the Dolphin (of which you will herewith receive a copy) or of the Tract of any former Navigators in Pursuits of the like kind; You are therefore in Pursuance of His Majesty's Pleasure hereby requir'd and directed to put to Sea with the Bark you Command so soon as the Observation of the Transit of the Planet Venus shall be finished .... You are to proceed to the southward in order to make discovery of the Continent above-mentioned until you arrive in the Latitiude of 40 degrees, unless you sooner fall in with it.

But not having discover'd it or any Evident signs of it in that Run, you are to proceed in search of it to the Westward between the Latitude before mentioned and the Latitude of 35 degrees until you discover it, or fall in with the Eastern side of the Land discover'd by Tasman and now called New Zealand.'

Cook travelled to Tahiti, where the Transit was observed and fresh stores were taken aboard. From there he went to New Zealand where he mapped the whole of the coastline and then sailed to the west and north until be came upon the south coast of Australia. On 29 April 1770 the *Endeavour* sailed into a natural harbour, which because of the abundance of plant life that proved to be a delight to the experts on Cook's ship was named Botany Bay. Botany Bay was just a few miles south of the modern Sydney and the area would become the home for thousands of convicts who would soon be despatched from Britain to found a new colony in the southern hemisphere.

Despite visiting all of the east coast of Australia, Cook remained largely ignorant of the actual size of the subcontinent, and though he undertook two more voyages before being killed in Hawaii in 1779, the nearest he came to Australia subsequently was a brief stop in Southern Tasmania in 1777. Cook is recognised as being one of the best navigators of any age and is also remembered for saving the lives of countless sailors by his policy of forcing them to eat citrus fruit and sauerkraut, thus ensuring they did not get scurvy, a terrible vitamin deficiency illness that was usually fatal.

James Cook claimed Australia for Britain, which was always looking for ports of call in various places around the globe. Ably assisted by the young Sir Joseph Banks, a rich and eager young botanist, Cook had demonstrated that the new lands would prove ideal for colonisation.

So it was that a large fleet of eleven ships set sail from Portsmouth in May 1787, bound for Botany Bay.[41] The expedition was captained by Arthur Phillips and apart from the seamen it comprised 717 convicts, of which 180 were women. These were guarded by 191 marines under 19 officers. The ships were also loaded with supplies and farming implements, with the intention of founding a colony that might eventually attract settlers other than those who had been forced to undertake the journey against their will.

The first fleet arrived intact on 18 January 1788 but Captain Phillips deemed Botany Bay unsuitable for the intended colony. As a result he sailed just a little further north and made his landfall in what would eventually come to be known as Sydney Harbour.

At the time, the prisons of Britain were filled to overflowing. Before the American war of independence, convicts had been sent to the New World, so with this destination now closed to the British authorities, Australia proved to be a godsend. Unfortunately the prisoners did not take naturally to farming and the whole colony faced severe difficulties until the arrival of the second fleet in 1790. Nevertheless, after a very shaky start things began to look better. The newcomers came to understand the climate and growing potential of the area and a European settled Australia became a reality.

---

41 *The First Fleet: The Convict Voyage That Founded Australia 1787-88*, Johnathan King, Macmillan, 1982

The region in which Sydney was located was named New South Wales and with a promise of a new life and free land it wasn't long before settlers other than convicts were taking passage to this huge new territory. At the same time British sights were set on New Zealand and the first Church Minister to preach a sermon there is a man who plays an important part in our story.

Samuel Marsden was born in the village of Farsley in West Yorkshire, which has now been swallowed up by the City of Leeds. Farsley sits on the edge of the Aire Valley, only a few miles from the ruins of Kirkstall Abbey, where our story began. Samuel was at first an apprentice blacksmith but he showed early educational promise and expressed a desire to join the Church. With the support of local bigwigs he managed to get a scholarship to a college of divinity and was ordained in 1793. At the suggestion of the politician William Wilberforce, Marsden agreed to take the role of assistant chaplain to the penal colony in New South Wales. Complete with a new wife, Elisabeth Friston, he arrived at Sydney in March 1794.[42]

Samuel Marsden was a real paradox of a man. He is probably one of the most hated individuals from early Australian history, mainly because of his highhanded manner and his habit of flogging the convict settlers within an inch of their life. He was particularly prejudiced against Catholics and especially against the Irish. He could be deeply intolerant, petulant, spiteful and self-serving. Despite all of this he is remembered with affection in New Zealand, where he took a real shine to the Maori inhabitants of the Islands. He was the first minister to preach a sermon in New Zealand and for all of his life he fought tenaciously to maintain the rights of the Maori over the European settlers.

What really incenses some Australians, even today, is the fact that although Marsden was such a dislikeable and even sadistic man, he was at least partly responsible for creating the circumstances that led Australia to its eventual greatness as a nation. The reason for this lies in Marsden's fondness for farming and his particular

---

42   *The Fatal Shore: History of the Transportation of Convicts to Australia*, 1787-1868, Robert Hughes, The Harvill Press, 1996

regard for sheep, though he saw both as a means to an end and was most interested in increasing his own fortune. He soon became an extremely wealthy landowner, farming at Parramatta, close to Sydney. [43]

Marsden had grown up in the Aire Valley of West Yorkshire and was well aware of the hardy sheep that were raised in the region. These animals had been bred for centuries to withstand the extremes of temperature necessary for survival in the changeable climate of the North of England. He had some Yorkshire sheep with him in Australia, probably the breed known as Swaledales, and on a subsequent trip back to England he managed to procure some Merino sheep from the royal flock belonging to the king. He certainly wasn't the only individual bringing sheep into Australia, but he showed a lifelong desire to improve the local flocks and to breed them to become better adapted to Australian life. Without realising it at the time Marsden's name can also be added to those who were directly responsible for the Industrial Revolution back in Britain, and all because of his contacts in his home village of Farsley.

Two of the men who had formerly been local merchants for the piece making of cloth in and around Farsley had been Rubin Gaunt and Abimalech Hainsworth. It is obvious from Gaunt's name that he came originally from Flemish stock because Gaunt would originally have been 'Gent', the name of a substantial textile town in Flanders. Unique amongst many of their contemporaries, Gaunt and Hainsworth could see the way the wind was blowing as far as textiles were concerned. They knew that the cottage industry was dying and that industrialisation was the way forward.

Late in the 18th century both Gaunt and Hainsworth opened woollen textile mills in Farsley and were soon involved in a competition and a personal animosity that would last for decades. Both men became rich but only after a very difficult time as the end of the 18th century approached. The problem they faced, together

---

43 *Samuel Marsden, the Great Survivor*, A T Yarwood, Melbourne University Press, 1996

with many dozens of other early mill owners, was one that seemed insurmountable for a while – they could not obtain sufficient raw wool to keep their new mills at peak output.[44]

The difficulty was primarily due to the foreign policies and personal caprices of one man – the Emperor Napoleon Bonaparte. Bonaparte had gained power in France at the end of the French Revolution, a terrible and bloody interlude in the country's history. Having risen through the ranks of the Revolutionary Army, Napoleon showed a genius and a thirst for power that were unequalled in his day and he crowned himself Emperor of France in 1804, though he had been in total control of the country for some years previous to this date.

Bonaparte was a superb general and began to carve out a large empire for France by conquering most of the countries in Western Europe. Unfortunately for him Britain did not capitulate to his wishes and since Britain was both a series of islands and also possessed a powerful navy, there was little that could be done about the situation. Napoleon's response to Britain's hatred of him and his regime was to impose a blockade on any exports destined for Britain from Continental ports and he also forbade exports from Britain to be landed in Western Europe.[45] The blockade commenced in 1807 and continued, with more or less success, until around 1812. The whole woollen textile industry of Britain and especially England had become totally dependent on wool from Spain and other parts of Europe and the blockade spelled imminent disaster for mill owners such as Gaunt and Hainsworth, who had invested heavily in buildings and equipment.

Samuel Marsden had sent samples of his Australian wool to Rubin Gaunt as early as 1806. These had been stored in the warehouse of Nethercape Mill and were chanced upon in 1808. The wool was discovered to be of excellent quality and as quickly as possible Rubin Gaunt sent word to Marsden that he would take just as much wool as the colonies could produce.

44 *Progress in Pudsey*, Joseph Lawson, First Published 1187. This version Caliban Books, 1978

45 *The Napoleonic Empire (Studies in European History)*, Geoffrey Ellis, Palgrave Macmillan, 2003

By the time the Continental blockade was lifted, Australia was already beginning a love affair with wool that would catapult her to an unassailable position. Half way up Town Street, Farsley, is a memorial built in the 1930s to commemorate the part Samuel Marsden played in the early story of Australia. It occupies the site of his former home and carved onto the monument is a sheep's head – a fitting memorial to man who though flawed in terms of his nature, nevertheless helped to put Australia firmly on the map and also did much to assist his home village and his birth nation at the time of their greatest need.

Another man who might rightfully claim to have had a hand in the founding of Australia was John Macarthur, the son of a Plymouth woollen textile merchant. He was born in 1767 and had shipped out to Australia as a Naval Ensign in the second fleet, arriving in 1790, three years before Marsden. Macarthur's temperament seems to have had much in common with that of Marsden. He could be both volatile and quarrelsome, which hardly endeared him to his fellow officers, especially since he also possessed a persecution complex almost as large as New South Wales and saw plots being hatched against him from every side.

Macarthur spent significant periods of his life under house arrest or actually in prison but he still found time to look around himself and to recognise the potential that Australia held. He had been brought up close to the South Downs, where Defoe had seen flocks of sheep that had astounded him, and of course Macarthur also came from a family of woollen merchants. He seems to have begun raising sheep very soon after his arrival in Australia, but it was obvious that sheep hardy enough to withstand the oppressive heat of the place did not produce the quality of wool that was required back in Britain. Nevertheless Macarthur had a degree of success and was running at least 3,000 sheep by 1801, making him the biggest owner of sheep in Australia at the time.

By 1801 John Macarthur had managed to alienate himself from just about everyone who was responsible for governing the new colony and he even contrived to fall out with his own colonel, which ultimately led to a duel. The senior officer was wounded in the shoulder and Macarthur was court-martialled as a result. Fearing he might be acquitted by any jury composed of colonists, the authorities sent Macarthur back to Britain – but their plan to get rid of him once and for all backfired. Macarthur was wise enough to take with him some samples of Australian wool and he arrived in London at precisely the time the Continental blockade was starting to bite. The frantic government was pleased to have a new source of raw wool from anywhere and reacted accordingly. Not only was Macarthur acquitted of all charges but he was sent back to Australia with a consignment of Merino sheep from the king's specimen herd and was granted 2,000 acres of land around Mount Taurus, by the Nepean River. This area was already recognised as being the finest pasture available in Australia at the time.

Before setting off back to Australia Macarthur packed his Merinos aboard a converted whaling ship he had purchased. Quite appropriately as things turned out he renamed the ship *The Golden Fleece* and with his prized sheep cosseted throughout the journey, he reached Australia in 1805.

Macarthur was not the first to bring Merinos to Australia. Marsden already possessed some, as did another early sheep breeder in the colony whose name was Jack Palmer, but Macarthur was certainly more successful than most in his efforts at crossbreeding.

The pure bred Merino is still recognised as being the best wool producer of all domestic sheep but it is a difficult animal to keep. Two centuries ago matters were even worse and some said you only had to look at a Merino in the wrong way for it to keel over and die. The breed was subject to disease, did not always lamb successfully, and didn't really have the stomach for Australian grass. What Macarthur did was to cross the Merino with Bengal and Afrikaner fat-tailed sheep, both breeds that were extremely hardy and which could take the heat. The result was interbred with various examples of English sheep and though the result looked very like a pedigree Merino, it was far better suited to life down under.

Although John Macarthur is credited with having been primarily responsible for the breed of sheep upon which Australia's prosperity would eventually rest, the accolade probably ought to go to his wife

Elizabeth. John was either in prison, or back and forth to England for so much of their married life, it was the long-suffering Elizabeth who actually ran the sheep farm and who saw to the experiments in breeding that would prove so successful.

John Macarthur was certainly not a man of letters but the Rev Samuel Marsden was. Throughout his whole life he was an inveterate letter writer. Some of his communications found their way to a couple of individuals whose own efforts towards achieving better, more productive sheep, were monumental. The first of these men was Sir Joseph Banks, the wealthy aristocratic naturalist who had accompanied Captain Cook on his first voyage of discovery to Australia. [46]

Joseph Banks was, during his long life, a virtual phenomenon. Born in London in 1743, he was educated at Harrow, Eton and then Oxford University, where he discovered his love of botany. After travelling to Newfoundland and Labrador, Banks enlisted with Cook in 1768 and proved to be an invaluable member of the expedition. He might have accompanied Cook again but at the death of his father he inherited the substantial family estates, which took up a great deal of his time. All the same, he kept in touch with Cook and showed great interest in the Pacific voyages, and in particular in Australia. Always a man of science Banks became president of the Royal Society of London in 1778, a position he would hold until his death in 1820.

Often using his own money, Banks sent botanists and naturalists all over the world to collect specimens for the collection at Kew Gardens, London, with which he had a close association. It was partly at his suggestion that the penal colonies in Australia were founded but he also encouraged other settlers to go there and he closely followed the gradual rise of Australia as something more than a convenient prison for Britain's criminal classes.

There was no aspect of the natural world that was beneath Banks'

---

46 *The Life of Sir Joseph Banks*, Edward Smith, University Press of the Pacific, 2002
Sir Joseph Banks, Charles Lyte, David and Charles, 1980
The Letters of Sir Joseph Banks: A Selection, 1768-1820, Joseph Banks, Edited Neil Chambers, Imperial College Press, 2001

interest and he was especially fond of farming. He lived at a time during which management of the land was undergoing a revolution of its own. During his lifetime ever more land was being enclosed and much of this was taken up for sheep rearing. With his intimate contacts in Australia, Banks became virtually obsessed with creating a sheep that could withstand the heat encountered there, whilst at the same time producing the finest possible wool. He experimented with crossbreeds that combined the stamina and hardiness of English sheep with the quality of fleece found in the Merino. During these experiments, which lasted for years, he regularly communicated with Samuel Marsden but his chief communicant on the subject was a man whose name has virtually disappeared from the annals of history. This is unfortunate because Sir John Sinclair is one of the most interesting characters the 18th century produced.[47]

John Sinclair was born in Thurso, Scotland in 1754 and was the heir to vast estates north of the border. From a very early age he showed himself to be an intelligent and capable administrator, with a wide-ranging mind and a multitude of interests that he followed throughout his life. Sinclair was, above all else, a liberal social reformer, though many of his excellent ideas were hijacked by people with no social conscience whatsoever, often to Sir John's great sorrow.

Spending as much time as possible on his Scottish estates, Sinclair was very much aware of the poverty and hardship of the Highlanders. He sought to address some of their difficulties and in particular he had a great hatred for a group of people known as 'tackmen'. The tackmen were individuals who rented large tracts of land from absentee Scottish landowners and then sublet small parcels of the land to local families. Generally speaking the smallholdings were not viable, partly because of their size but also because of inefficient farming practices.

Sir John did not allow tackmen anywhere near his own land and he sought to do all he could to make the Highland farmers

---

47 *Agricultural Sir John: The life of Sir John Sinclair of Ulbster, 1754-1835*, Rosalind Mitchison, Bles Publishing, 1962

more efficient and therefore more prosperous. This did involve some relocation in order to create larger farms but Sinclair never evicted a single tenant and always found those displaced new homes and work on his estates. In particular he recognised the value of sheep to the Highlands. He noted that:

'The Highlands of Scotland may sell, at present, perhaps from £200,000 to £300,000 worth of lean cattle per annum. The same ground will produce twice as much mutton, and there is wool into the bargain. If covered with the coarse-woolled breed of sheep, the wool might be worth about £300,000, the value of which can only be doubled by the art of the manufacturer; whereas the same ground under the Cheviot or True Mountain breed will produce at least £900,000 of fine wool.'

As a result he worked tirelessly, often in association with Sir Joseph Banks, to create crossbred sheep that could produce good wool and yet survive on the inhospitable Highland mountain slopes. Sir John Sinclair was also in communication with Samuel Marsden in Australia and made suggestions to both Marsden and Banks regarding blood- lines and breeding techniques for Australia.

Sir John Sinclair had a tremendous part to play in the improvement of agriculture, not just in Scotland but across the whole of the British Isles. At the insistence of the prime minister of his day, he single-handedly created the Department of Agriculture, being a member of parliament and a minister in the government led by William Pitt the Younger. Sinclair was also on good terms with the monarch and was given many Merino sheep from the Royal herd. He was fortunate enough to live during the long reign of King George III, a rather sad character for protracted periods of his time on the throne because he suffered from bouts of apparent madness. Nevertheless George was particularly interested in land management and as a result he acquired the nickname of 'Farmer George'.

Sinclair and the king became firm friends and co-operated with regard to sheep breeding, with the result that new strains of crossbred sheep soon began to appear on Sinclair's Scottish lands. These were a tremendous success and made Sir John even richer – money that he unselfishly ploughed back into the welfare of his tenants. Unfortunately, not all Scottish landlords were nearly as generous or forward looking and Sir John Sinclair's greatest claim to fame is that he inadvertently instigated bigger Highland clearances than had ever taken place before.[48]

Worst amongst these have to be those known as the Sutherland Clearances, so named because the land in question was owned by the Countess of Sutherland. Her agents began their clearances in Strathnavar in 1814, by which time Sir John Sinclair's experiments in sheep breeding and his new Highland farming methods were quite clearly paying handsome dividends that others wished to emulate for the sake of their own purses. The agents of the Countess ordered tenants from their homes, which they immediately burned and demolished to prevent any possibility of the people returning. How many people were dispossessed in Assynt, Caithness, Dornoch, Rogort, Loth, Clyne and Kildonan will never be known. The land was then enclosed and sheep took the place of the farmers.

The displaced smallholders were offered pitifully small patches of land near the barren and desolate seashore. How they were to earn a living so far from all they had known for generations was not really an issue as far as the Countess or her hit men were concerned. Many starved and still more found ways and means to leave their native land forever. Some went to the cities of England and others shipped across the Atlantic to either the US or Canada. Still more took the even longer journey to Australia and in later clearances to New Zealand.

This was a pitiful episode in the history of Scotland and it has never been forgotten, particularly in Highland regions. Hatred of absentee landlords remains strong and helps to fund the calls for Scottish independence and total home rule.

Progress is a remorseless master and the inequities of the past can never be redressed in the present. In the end the misery of those Scottish families proved to be the oil that lubricated the wheels of industry. In England, the greatest revolution the world had ever known was about to take place. The fuel for the furnace

---

48   *The Highland Clearances*, John Prebble, Penguin Books, 1969

of mechanisation was wool – thousands and thousands of tons of fleeces, brought down from the mountains of Scotland and carried by carts from the hills and valleys of England and Wales. More bales were brought up through the Bay of Biscay from Spain and others found their way to Britain along the routes of the wool clippers, a new type of fast merchant ships that raced back and forth, to and from Australia.

The opening up of New Zealand offered yet another supplier of good quality wool and one with a far more temperate climate than existed across much of Australia. The British were actually very slow to recognise the value of New Zealand as a potential colony. For one thing it was already inhabited, and whilst the Aboriginal peoples of Australia had proved to be no real handicap to the formation of a European Australia, the Maori of New Zealand were a very different matter. The Maori were Polynesians who had arrived in New Zealand from the Pacific around 1000 AD. Abel Tasman, the very first European to set foot on New Zealand found to his cost that the Maori could be a very warlike people and after a bloody encounter, he treated them with the greatest respect.

For the next one and a half centuries Europeans showed little interest in New Zealand but by the 1790s missionaries were visiting the place, as were whaling ships and a few traders. What spurred British colonization was the fact that they became aware of French plans to establish colonies in South Island. The Maori were prevailed upon to sign a treaty with the British in 1840, though they did so very much on their own terms, which is why the Maori have never suffered as a result of colonization in the same way that was the unfortunate lot of indigenous Australian peoples. Not that all went well between the Maori and the influx of settlers that soon arrived. Between 1845 and 1872 there was a series of skirmishes and pitched battles that became known as the New Zealand Wars. During this time the Maori proved to be a formidable foe and although New Zealand was eventually fully colonized, Maori rights and privileges remain paramount to the governing of the Islands even today.

Much of the fighting in the 1850s and 1860s took place in North Island and the Maori in South Island showed a much greater willingness to either sell or lease land. Thousands of sheep were shipped across from Australia and flourished there. New Zealand has a climate not unlike that of Great Britain and the sheep obviously felt very much at home. There were problems at first, not least of all repeated outbreaks of sheep scab, a terrible disease that killed thousands of sheep. In addition the European rabbit, which had also been brought to New Zealand, began to breed uncontrollably, forcing many settlers from their land.

Eventually these problems were overcome and modern New Zealand has more sheep per head of human population than anywhere else on earth. There are presently about ten sheep for every human, with 360,000 flocks across both islands.

Even before the founding of the colonies in New Zealand, Britain was embarking on a great journey and it would soon drag much of the rest of the world with it – towards a future that was at one and the same time frightening and exciting. Nothing like this had ever happened before on the planet. It would lead humanity towards forms of technology that could never have been dreamed of during the 18th century.

Strangely enough, with the exception of the bat family, the first mammal to leave the ground and soared into the air at the same time as the Industrial Revolution was starting to bite – but it wasn't a human being. In 1783, as Sir Joseph Banks was working hard on his ancestral lands and also as president of the Royal Society, and whilst Australia was first being colonized by Europeans, two men in France were experimenting with hot air balloons. They were the Montgolfier brothers, Joseph and Etienne. Late in the summer of 1783 they launched a balloon with three passengers – a duck, a chicken and a sheep! By November of the same year the passengers in the gondola of the balloon were men but the unnamed French sheep had soared up into the clouds first and had returned safe and sound. Vive le Mouton!

All steamed up

As the 18th century advanced, new water-powered textile mills were springing up in many places, but West Yorkshire and Lancashire were attracting more than any other region of the British Isles. The main reasons for this seem to have been the fact that textile creation was already established in the region and that the necessary geological conditions were present (i.e. fast-running streams carrying lime-free water). In the case of cotton, Lancashire had another edge because of its moist climate. This is the main reason why although woollen textiles continued to be made in significant quantities in East Anglia and the West Country well into the 19th century, cotton never moved from Lancashire to any great extent.

What really made the North of England the centre for textile manufacture once the Industrial Revolution gained pace was also a matter of geology. As Daniel Defoe had noted at the beginning of the 18th century, the region was rich in coal that could be readily accessed using relatively small bell pits. The presence of coal would eventually be a crucial factor.

Gradually the different areas of Britain began to take on a higher degree of specialisation than had formerly been the case. For example, parts of the Midlands, as with Yorkshire and Lancashire, had significant coal seams but they also had iron ore. As early as 1709 Abraham Darby, from Shropshire, had discovered how to use coke rather than charcoal in the process of smelting metal.[49]

49 *The Most Extraordinary District in the World: Ironbridge and Coalbrookdale*, editor Barrie Trinder, Phillimore and Co Ltd, 1988

This was important, not least because reliable supplies of charcoal were getting harder to find, at least near to the areas where iron ore was also available. The use of coke, which involved driving impure gases from coal, revolutionised the smelting of metal ores and coal was readily available close to where Abraham Darby was already working.

Brass and iron foundries began to spring up around the Midlands, supplying the raw materials the metal workers of burgeoning centres such as Birmingham required to satisfy ever-growing markets. The woollen textile trade, once so important around Birmingham and Coventry, slowly began to be overtaken by the needs of both light and heavy engineering.

Meanwhile Cornwall, down in the very south west of England, was going from strength to strength on the back of the one invaluable raw material it possessed. This was tin. Although tin had been mined in Cornwall as far back in time as the Bronze Age, the needs of industrialisation dramatically increased the amount demanded. Tin is mixed with copper to create bronze, a metal that was invaluable to industrialisation.[50]

It was because of the needs of the Cornish tin miners that the next crucial step towards ultimate industrialisation was taken. One major problem was that in order to find good seams of tin, the Cornish miners had to dig deep shafts, far deeper than the coalmines of the North and Midlands. These were inclined to fill with water very quickly and draining the water from them was proving to be a nightmare. All sorts of solutions were tried, for example horses turning great wheels that ran pumps, but nothing really answered the needs of the miners until a man by the name of Thomas Newcomen turned his attention to creating a machine that would pump hundreds of gallons every hour.[51]

Newcomen was an ironmonger. He was born in Dartmouth, Cornwall, in 1663 and grew up in an area that relied totally on tin

50 *The Early British Tin Mines*, Sandy Gerrard, Tempus Publishing, 2000
51 *Thomas Newcomen: The Prehistory of the Steam Engine*, LTC Rolt, David and Charles, 1963

mining. Because of his chosen trade he was more aware than most of the problems created by flooded mines and he began to look seriously at the problem. There was already one machine available that had showed a certain amount of promise. This was an engine created by another local man, Thomas Savery. His machine, called 'the Miner's Friend', used steam to create a vacuum that directly drew water from a flooded mine. In its own way it was an ingenious idea but it was hopelessly inefficient.[52]

Newcomen came up with a different idea. Like Savery he recognised the power of a vacuum but he used steam to create his vacuum inside a cylinder. The piston that ran in the cylinder was connected to a lever, or beam, that transferred the energy from the piston to the pump mechanism in the mine. Newcomen's 'Beam Engine' as it came to be called, was still only 1% efficient but it achieved its purpose. The first example was installed, not in Cornwall, but at Dudley Castle in Staffordshire, where from 1712 it kept a coalmine free of water. The engine had a cylinder 21 inches in diameter and around 8 feet in length. It ran at 12 strokes a minute and was capable of lifting 10 gallons of water with each stroke from a depth of 156 feet.

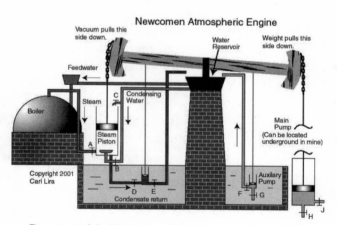

Drawing of the Newcomen Atmospheric or Beam Engine

---

52 *Miner's Friend, Thomas Savery*, Antiquarian Facsimiles, 1979

By the time Thomas Newcomen died in 1729 there were at least 100 of his engines working throughout Britain and on the Continent. Unfortunately the patent Savery already possessed was deemed to apply to Newcomen's Beam Engine, even though it was radically different. This meant that in order to produce the Beam Engine Newcomen had to go into partnership with Savery. Like many inventors he was not a good businessman and never made much money from his creation. Primitive the Beam Engine may have been but no matter how inefficient it was, it is a mark of respect to its robust construction that an example in Barnsley, Yorkshire, was still working as recently as 1934.

Although the Beam Engine was ideal for the needs of pumping water from mines, it was too bulky to be applied to other purposes. What was needed was a more efficient steam engine that could be smaller and yet still supply sufficient power for its purpose. This came courtesy of James Watt, the son of a merchant who was born in Greenock, Scotland in 1736.[53] Watt would be the first of many fine engineers who came from Scotland and he started his career as an instrument maker in Glasgow. He soon proved his worth on projects far bigger than instruments and in 1763 he was asked to repair a broken Newcomen Beam Engine. He soon began to realise just how inefficient the Newcomen engine was and devised a system whereby the used steam was cooled in a condenser separate from the main cylinder. The result was an engine of far greater power and one that could be made considerably smaller.

James Watt was far from wealthy and so he joined forces with John Roebuck, the wealthy owner of a Scottish ironworks. Roebuck had not made his initial money from iron. He started his career as a physician and conducted chemical experiments in his spare time. What made him wealthy was a method of producing dilute acids cheaply. These were used extensively in the woollen trade to bleach cloth. Prior to Roebuck's discovery, sour milk had been used, which was far from ideal and very smelly!

---

53 *Watt's Perfect Engine: Steam and the Age of Invention*, Ben Marsden, Icon Books, 2002

Roebuck financed James Watt's development of the steam engine until 1773, when there was a depression in industry that forced him into bankruptcy. Watt needed another backer and as luck would have it he came across Matthew Boulton, a wealthy coin maker and the son of a silversmith from Birmingham.[54] Whereas Watt's engines up to this time had been similar to those of Newcomen, in that they worked via a beam and so were ideal for pumping, the next innovation had to be a rotary engine. Boulton and Watt sold many examples of the refined beam engine, which was four times more efficient than Newcomen's engine. The later Boulton and Watt engine, which used a system of gears to turn the up-and-down movements of the beam engine into rotary motion, was perfected by 1781.

Boulton and Watt set up a factory in Soho, Birmingham, where the now fully developed steam engine was refined and finally produced. This was a 'double acting engine' because Watt had made it possible to use the steam cylinder to drive the piston in both directions. In 1783 the first Boulton and Watt steam engine was installed in a textile mill. In the years that followed, cotton and woollen textile manufacturers clamoured for the Boulton and Watt engines, of which well over 500 were built.

The Boulton and Watt engines were used for a variety of purposes and many are still running to this day but nowhere did they have a greater impact than in West Yorkshire and Lancashire. Steam power was far more efficient and reliable than water wheels. Fuel was no problem because the whole of West Yorkshire and large parts of Lancashire were rich in coal seams and coal was the ideal fuel to heat the boiler of a steam engine. Textile mills began to be built in valley bottoms instead of in places where fast-flowing streams had been the deciding factor. Cities such as Bradford in West Yorkshire started to flourish, whilst existing places of importance to the woollen trade, for example Halifax and Leeds, ceased to be simply towns where merchants came to sell their cloth – now they

---

54 *The Lunar Men: A Story of Science, Art, Invention and Passion*, Jenny Uglow, Faber and Faber, 2002

started to sport large mills of their own and to grow exponentially as a result.

What followed was little short of miraculous. Fortunately for the manufacturers, the population was rising at an unprecedented rate and as more and more enclosures drove people from their land, they began to move into the towns in great numbers. The English workforce was swelled by Scots and Irish who were also being driven from their ancestral homes.

There is still a great argument amongst historians as to whether enclosure brought people to the towns, where they became involved in the new industries, or whether the industries themselves 'drew' people in from surrounding areas. The truth of the matter is that both explanations of what happened are equally valid. Cities such as Manchester increased their population by 1,000% between 1801 and 1851, even though the national population had only grown by 100%. The same was true for towns and cities such as Liverpool, Sheffield, Birmingham and Leeds. By 1851 for the first time in history there were more people in Britain living in towns and cities than in the country.

Much of what was taking place had been made possible because of Boulton and Watt's steam engines but once the race for technology had begun to gain pace, Boulton and Watt actually 'suppressed' new developments. This was particularly the case in terms of the transport infrastructure. Britain was gradually growing into an industrial giant but the nature of its topography made the movement of goods from factories to ports and from town to town extremely difficult. Those same areas in the north, where wool and cotton were being worked in such large quantities, were hilly places with terrible roads and rivers that simply were not navigable. Canals played an important part in some cases but canal transport through the uplands was slow. What was needed was an entirely new system of getting both goods and people from A to B and the first step in a solution to this problem came from the coal mines.

For centuries it had been realised that horses could pull bigger loads on specifically designed track-ways, and that they would be even more efficient if carts were placed on wooden rails, thus ironing out the lumps and bumps of a conventional roadway. This was particularly appropriate in the case of the sort of coalmine known as a 'drift mine' in which a horizontal shaft is driven straight into a hillside, with no or very little inclination. If trucks or carts ran on wooden rails the amount of weight the average horse could put was much greater than would have been possible using a conventional cart running on the ground.

Some quite long track-ways of this sort already existed by the middle of the 18th century but they still relied on human or horsepower in order to shift loads from one place to another. Enter a man called Richard Trevithick,[55] a giant in every sense of the word. Standing well over six feet tall and strong enough to write his name on a beam six feet from the floor, with a weight of half a hundredweight hanging from his thumb, Trevithick made an impression on everyone he met.

Born in Illogan, Cornwall in 1771, the young Richard soon showed an aptitude for engineering. He was familiar with both Newcomen and Boulton and Watt steam engines but thought that both could be improved, primarily by stepping up the pressure at which they worked. He modified steam engines used in tin mines but his ultimate desire was to make a steam engine small enough and yet powerful enough to travel along the road, like a stagecoach. By Christmas Eve 1801 his prototype was ready and he set off with friends along the country roads near his home. His steam carriage, known as the 'Puffing Devil', worked well, until Richard and his friends abandoned it to call at a local hostelry. The beer flowed freely and by the time they returned to the Puffing Devil, they discovered that it had overheated and caught fire.

After many disappointments and setbacks Trevithick was eventually introduced to Samuel Homfray, the owner of an ironworks in Merthyr Tydfil, Wales. The ironworks already had a track-way and it was one made of iron rather than wood. This was ideal for Trevithick's purpose and in 1804 he constructed a locomotive, with

---

55   *Richard Trevithick: The Man and His Machines*, Anthony Burton, Aurum Press, 2000

a high-pressure boiler, to pull a load along the track. This, the first true locomotive ever built, was named *Penydarren*. It only achieved three journeys before its weight broke the brittle iron rails on which it has been built to run. Nevertheless it did pull sizeable loads and managed a stately five miles per hour.

Joining the list of those inventors without whom the Industrial Revolution could never have taken place, but who never made anything from their efforts, Richard Trevithick eventually died in extreme poverty in 1833. However, not only had he built the world's first steam locomotive, he also briefly ran the world's first passenger railway. In the summer of 1808 he had built a new locomotive, called *Catch Me Who Can*. He created a circular track around Euston Square in London and charged one shilling to anyone who wanted to take a ride in one of the carriages pulled by the locomotive.

Richard Trevithick's 1808 locomotive 'Catch Me Who Can'

This locomotive encountered the same problem as his earlier models in that it was so heavy it broke its own rails. It would be some time before it was realised that only rails made from wrought rather than cast iron would take such loads.

Many people experimented with steam-powered locomotives both during and after the life of Richard Trevithick but they all came up against one insurmountable problem. Boulton and Watt had tied up every possible patent in the design of their own engines. They were not willing to grant licences to other inventors and neither would they experiment with high-pressure boilers themselves, which they considered to be potentially lethal. The patents finally expired in 1801 and the road was open for a new breed of steam engine.

Our next contender for the maker of the Industrial Revolution takes us back to the woollen trade and to Leeds. In 1805 a young engineer by the name of Matthew Murray[56] was working for a company in which he was a partner. The name of the company was Fenton, Murray and Wood. Murray had been born in Newcastle upon Tyne in 1765, into a family of woollen workers. Once qualified as an engineer he obtained work in Leeds designing a flax-spinning machine, something that had never been achieved before his time.

By 1810 he had met John Blenkinsop, a man who owned a colliery in Middleton, just a few miles to the south of Leeds. Leeds was growing rapidly at the time. Textile mills within the town were hungry for coal, which was also needed for the domestic fires of the workers. Blenkinsop already had a track-way leading from his pithead to Leeds Bridge, but the cost of hauling coal carts by horses was proving prohibitive. Together Murray and Blenkinsop created four locomotives. The most successful of these was called *Salamanca*. It did not run on conventional track but was the first 'track' railway. The track was 'toothed' and the wheels of the locomotive were made to run within the teeth, thus 'pulling' the locomotive and its load along. A similar principle has often been used on mountain railways, where adhesion is a problem.

The four locomotives between them replaced the 50 horses and 200 men that had previously been needed to haul coal from Middleton to Leeds. Despite a few technical problems, again related to the track rather than the locomotive, the Middleton Railway used the Murray locomotives until 1835. The Middleton Railway had been licensed by Act of Parliament as early as 1758 and it had become the world's first steam hauled commercial railway in 1812. The more famous Stockton to Darlington Railway is generally

---

56 *Matthew Murray: Pioneer Engineer*, E Kilburn Scott, TEE Publishing, 1999

quoted as having been the first true steam railway but Middleton was already in existence 13 years before the Stockton to Darlington Railway became a reality.

Would the world's first truly successful steam locomotive, the *Salamanca*, ever have been built without the importance to West Yorkshire of wool? It is unlikely. John Blenkinsop's coalmine existed to supply the mills and houses of Leeds, which was a town utterly dependent on wool and its ancillary trades. Matthew Murray could never have come to Leeds as a young engineer if it were not for wool, and in any case he had been born into a wool workers family himself. Of course, historians still insist on referring to the Stockton to Darlington railway as being the first in the world and it certainly was the first successful passenger railway ever constructed. Without the Stockton to Darlington Railway, James Stephenson, the greatest of all the locomotive engineers and a man who built many of Britain's railways, may never have been anything more than a bit player in history. Readers may be interested to learn that the Stockton to Darlington Railway also owed its existence to wool and therefore ultimately to the sheep.[57]

The Stockton to Darlington Railway was the brainchild of one man. His name was Edward Pease, a Quaker whose family had originally come from South Yorkshire. Edward Pease was born in Darlington in the year 1767. His father was a successful wool merchant of the sort that had kept the cottage industry supplied for so many decades. Despite some wealth already existing in the family Edward left school at 14 years of age to join the family business. In addition to their interest in wool, the Pease family had already emulated the Medici of Italy by turning the white gold that was wool into the more usual sort accrued through banking. This had begun in 1761, the brainchild of Joseph Pease, father of Edward.

During many years spent travelling around the district where he lived, delivering raw wool and collecting finished cloth, Edward Pease became aware of the shortcomings of transportation in the

---

57   *The Origins of Railway Enterprise: The Stockton and Darlington Railway 1821–1863*, Maurice W Kirby, Cambridge University Press, 2002

England of his time. In particular he thought that there was a definite call for a railroad upon which horses could be used to deliver coal from the mines at West Durham to the port of Stockton. With increasing wealth and a determination to push forward the bounds of the possible, Edward Pease was instrumental in forming a new company, together with other businessmen from his area. This was named The Stockton and Darlington Railway Company. It came into existence in 1821.

An Act of Parliament was necessary to construct such a long track-way and this was passed on 19 April 1821. It was at about the same time that Edward Pease met Nicholas Wood, the manager of Killingworth Colliery. Wood had been impressed by an engineer called George Stephenson[58] and together the two men suggested to Pease that the new railway would be much more efficient if it used steam locomotives, rather than horses. Stephenson claimed he could build the necessary locomotives.

George Stephenson had very humble origins. He was the son of a colliery fireman from a village close to Newcastle upon Tyne. As a very small boy George was employed as a cowherd but he showed a real interest in machines of all kinds and eventually became a colliery engineman. His only son, Robert, who would also prove to be a wonderful engineer, was born in 1803. Robert would grow to help his father at every stage of the evolution of locomotives and railways.

George Stephenson was 27 years old when he gained the position of engineman at Killingworth Colliery and during weekends he took the primitive steam engines already at the colliery to pieces, the better to understand how they worked. By 1812 George Stephenson had amassed so much knowledge that he was upgraded to the post of enginewright. In the years that followed he took note of other engineers who were trying to develop locomotives for use in the colliery business and he finally persuaded his employer to allow him to build a locomotive for the Killingworth Colliery. The result was

---

58 *George and Robert Stephenson: The Railway Revolution*, L.T.C. Rolt, Penguin Books, 1988

the *Blutcher*, the first successful flanged-wheel steam locomotive ever constructed.

So impressed with the locomotive was Nicholas Wood that he and Stephenson made the approach to Edward Pease, who went to Killingworth to see the *Blutcher* and other examples of Stephenson engines at work. He had to agree that steam power was the way forward and convinced his fellow directors that this was the case.

A new Act of Parliament was required in order to build a steam-operated railway and this was obtained in 1823. At the same time Pease joined forces with another businessman by the name of Michael Longdridge, George Stephenson and his son Robert to create a company to build steam locomotives commercially. This was eventually called Robert Stephenson and Company and became the most famous locomotive factory in the world.

The first locomotive built for the Stockton and Darlington Railway was called *Locomotion*. In addition to hauling freight, it also pulled a passenger coach that had been christened *Experiment*. The train could achieve speeds of 15 miles per hour and it represented the first time in history that a railway had provided a regular passenger service – that is if we discount Trevithick's circular railway in London.

The next most famous railway from the early days of steam was that built between Liverpool and Manchester and opened in 1830. This was 31 miles in length and was also created with Quaker money. Its primary purpose was to transport goods of all sorts between the port of Liverpool and the industrial centre of Manchester. In particular the track would carry raw cotton to the mills and finished cloth back to the port.

Although there was supposed to be a competition in 1829 to see which of several locomotives would be purchased by the Liverpool and Manchester Railway this aspect of history is something of a myth. The whole competition was one of the world's first publicity stunts. Out of all the locomotives that were entered only five turned up and two of these were withdrawn on the day because of mechanical problems. Of the three that remained, that built by the Stephensons was by far and away the best. The dice was well and truly loaded in favour of the Stephensons from the start, who had, in addition to creating a brand new and revolutionary locomotive named *Rocket*, also surveyed and built the railway in its totality.

When the *Northumbrian*, another of Stephenson's locomotives, pulled the first passenger train into Manchester on 15 September 1830, it was pelted with stones by disgruntled cotton weavers. They didn't so much have an issue with the railway but rather with the Duke of Wellington, who was aboard one of the coaches. He had been involved in an incident some years earlier in which many workers had been killed by troops in what became known as the Peterloo Massacre.

In the years that followed Britain produced many fine railway engineers and once the technology began to be used elsewhere, the whole world took to the railways. The iron horse opened up the US, brought speedy connections between destinations in Europe and Asia and crossed the steaming jungles and baked plains of India. No doubt even without the Middleton Railway in Leeds, the Stockton to Darlington Railway or the line from Liverpool to Manchester, the locomotive would have been produced and developed sooner or later. Nevertheless it remains a fact that the first two railways were paid for by money earned as a direct result of the woollen trade, and the third rested on cotton, which only came to be used in Britain because of the textile expertise that already existed in Lancashire thanks to wool. In yet another major development that helped to build the modern world, we owe a debt of gratitude to the sheep.

All the colours of the rainbow

If there is one fact about which we can be certain, even from the remotest times, it is that human beings love colour. Cave paintings, for example those found in many areas of France and produced up to 20,000 years ago, depict wonderful scenes from Stone Age life. Horses, wild cattle and many other creatures familiar to our ancient ancestors have been reproduced in fantastic detail and the majority of them still show a muted version of the bright colours that the artists originally used. The discovery of deliberately collected pigments such as ochre in caves in South Africa extending back as much as 100,000 years is now starting to indicate that human fascination for colour is even older than we previously thought.

The early cave painters used whatever natural colours nature could provide. These would often be derived from various sorts of earth or rock, crushed down to a fine powder and then either mixed with water or animal fat. Some very bright hues can be created in this way but nature also provides colour in other forms. Plant material can often be quite rich in colour. Good examples are woad, a blue or even purple colour derived from the leaves of a common plant called *Isatis tinctoria* and madder, the botanical name of which is *Rubia tinctorum*, an Asiatic plant that provides a rich, red colour from its root.

Ancient people did not stop at creating works of art on cave walls, they were also fond of decorating their own bodies. Mummies from Siberia, in which the permafrost has preserved bodies many centuries old, provide examples of people whose bodies were tattooed in a veritable palette of colours and we also now know that tattooing also took place much further west. The body of an unfortunate man from the Copper Age, who breathed his last on a winter mountain pass in the Italian Alps was discovered some years ago. His body had been preserved by 'freeze-drying' and it sported a wealth of tattoos. We also know from Roman writers that at the time of Julius Caesar's excursion into Britain in 55BC, the locals were painting their bodies with blue woad, at least for purposes of ceremony and battle.

Exactly when people also began to apply colours to their clothing has to remain a matter of conjecture. The earliest definite examples we possess come from the wrappings of Egyptian mummies that date back over 5,000 years but the practice almost certainly goes back to a period long before this date. Unfortunately, all fabrics are somewhat fragile and do not tend to last well in archaeological sites but it is a fair bet that people who created such vibrant colours on cave walls and who also adorned their own bodies may have been colouring animal skins and fabrics for nearly as long as clothes have been worn.

All of this brings us to a very important part of our story and one that led not only to a brighter world for all of us but to the evolution of a chemical industry that owes much to a range of people across many centuries who have striven to make more colourful and permanent dyes for fabric.

Early dies for fabrics such as wool and linen were doubtless fairly unsuccessful, at least in terms of their ability to stay fixed to fabric once it was washed. Many plant, animal and mineral substances will die raw yarn of almost any sort in a variety of bright colours but these often fail to remain attached to the molecular structure of the fibre and readily fade or even disappear when water is introduced. There are basically two main types of dyes available. These are known as either substantive or adjective dyes. Substantive dyes, for example indigo, derived from a plant called 'Indigofera' and those derived from a range of lichens, become permanently attached to fabric and cannot be removed by washing. Adjective dies are different and if the colour they bring to fabric is to be retained, some other chemical agent is also necessary in order to 'fix' the dye. [59]

Plant fibres are made of cellulose and these almost always require chemical fixing of colour by way of a chemical agent that is known as a 'mordent'. The word mordent is Greek and means 'to bite'. Many substances have been used to prepare cloth to take natural dyes but the very best ones are metallic in nature, such as iron, aluminium or copper.

Many new dies were introduced to the West at the time of the Crusades, as early as the 11th century. New trade routes introduced by the Knights Templars and other agencies began to flourish, bringing more exotic dyes from places as far away as Turkey. These had been known in the East for centuries. A document from Greece, known as the Stockholm papyrus,[60] gives details of foodstuffs and dyes used in Egypt during the 3rd and 4th centuries and the nature of this document seems to demonstrate the dying techniques had been in place for hundreds if not thousands of years. The Stockholm papyrus details methods of dying using red, green and purple dyes, as well as indicating how dyes could be successfully fixed using alum, copper and iron oxides. Amongst the substances used for dyes were a plant known as 'alkanet' (*Anchusa tinctoria*) as well as sheep and camel urine, lentils, vinegar and barley malt. This exhaustive document also contains recipes for the use of woad, madder and kermes, which is made from the bodies of specific insects, and plants of the heliotrope family.

One of the most precious dyes ever known to humanity originated in the Mediterranean, well before the modern era. This was known as Tyrian purple[61] and was obtained from the mucous gland of a specific shellfish. The Phoenicians created colonies in places where the shellfish were to be found and traded the dye all across their

---

59 *Colors: The Story of Dyes and Pigments*, Francois Delamare, Bernard Guineau, Publisher Harry N Abrams, 2001

60 *The Alchemy Reader: From Hermes Trismegistus to Isaac Newton*, Stanton J Linden, Cambridge University Press, 2003

61 *Tyrian or Imperial Purple Dye: The Mystery of Imperial Purple Dye*, John Edmonds, Publisher John Edmonds, 2000

empire – at an extortionate price. A similar colour, though not so deep in hue, was also available to the Irish. This came from a different sort of shellfish, this time a member of the whelk family.

As Northern Italy began to gain ground in the creation of textiles and especially textile finishing, more and more substances used for dying began to arrive from the East. From locations such as Venice and Florence the dyes would then be transhipped to other parts of Europe, including London. Doubtless country-folk across most of the Continent would have settled for locally produced dyes, which provided fairly sober colours, but even prior to the 14th century there was a ready market for brightly coloured cloths, produced for the aristocracy and royalty. We know from laws passed by Parliament in England immediately after the Black Death that people who had no legal right to do so were showing a preference for exotic materials of very bright colours, so it is certain that these were available from a quite early date.

It is probable that one of the reasons why Britain did not develop its own finished textile trade earlier than it did was because of difficulties regarding the dying of cloth. The same was true in Flanders because much of the cloth that found its way down to the Champagne fairs from the 12th century on was not coloured at all and was transhipped to Italy, where the dyes people wanted to make their clothes bright and cheerful were more readily available. Gradually however the raw materials for dying did find their way to the centres of textile production other than Italy but in Britain especially another problem began to arise after the Reformation of the 16th century. This had as much to do with religion as it did with technology.

From earliest times alum, the major chemical used as a mordant until well into the 19th century, had been obtained from Turkey. The Italians controlled all the alum that came into Europe and charged high prices to supply it to other states. Good, alum-bearing rock was eventually found in Italy but it was in an area controlled by the Vatican. Successive popes were very protective of the alum monopoly and were certainly not willing to supply it to a country such as England that had abandoned the 'true faith'. Even when alum could be imported the cost was prohibitive, being around £53 a ton, which at the time was an amount that could have purchased an entire village. By the reign of Queen Elizabeth I (1533 – 1603) the gradually developing woollen textile trade of England was in great difficulties through lack of this one basic substance. So troubled was the Queen by this state of affairs that she invited certain 'chymists' from the Continent to come and settle in England in order to try and remedy the situation.

The first source of alum in England seems to have been exploited at least as early as 1595, in the village of Guisborough, not far from Middlesborough in North Yorkshire. Around this area there are exposed 'Jurassic shales' that contain alum, though the alum was extremely difficult to extract from the shale until comparatively recent times. Further alum works were gradually opened in the same general area and especially along the coast between the River Tees in the North and Whitby in the South. The need for alum was becoming more and more crucial as the 17th century dawned but what defies belief is how those extracting it finally hit upon the methods necessary. Chemistry was in its infancy and so we can only put the eventual procedure used down to trial and error.

The alum-bearing rock was dug from hillsides where there were good outcrops of the Jurassic shales. There were especially rich seams to be found close to the modern town of Saltburn and the little village of Robin Hood's Bay, both in North Yorkshire. Large quantities of shale would be dug and then placed above the tide-line of the beach, on fires made from brushwood and also larger logs brought from further away. The bonfires could be as high as 100 feet and when sufficient material had been added, they would be lit. It took months of smouldering for the first part of the process to take place. This happened when the toasted rock was 'calcined', which allowed the aluminium sulphate to be released. The calcined shale was now placed in huge pits and covered with fresh water, which had to be constantly replaced. Eventually, by transferring the water from one pit to another, it became steeped in aluminium sulphate. At this stage it was called 'alum liquor', and was ready for the next part of this complicated process.

The liquor was now taken to a purpose-built site – an early factory, called an Alum house. Once at the Alum house, which often involved significant journeys through wooden pipes and even tunnels, the liquor was boiled to drive off the water. The crystals of aluminium sulphate would only appear once alkali was added. In the early stages of the industry there was only one readily available supply of alkali and this came from human urine. So much urine was needed for the process that there wasn't nearly enough available locally, even though people were paid to supply it. Ultimately it had to be shipped up from London, no doubt a lucrative trade for the sailors concerned but certainly not a pleasant one.

Finally the alum crystals appeared and could be sold on to dye-houses all over the country, and even exported to other places that were not popular with the Pope. The price of alum fell to £26 a ton once the Yorkshire alum works were fully in operation and they also acted as an early spur to the coal trade because once the local supplies of wood ran out, coal was the only alternative for the huge bonfires necessary to calcine the shale. Coal was shipped down from Newcastle upon Tyne and arrived at the coastal port of Whitby, which on the strength of the alum trade turned itself from a village into a thriving town.

If alum making was a smelly business, dying wasn't much better. Queen Elizabeth I passed a law that said dye-houses had to be located at specified distances from villages and towns. Dyers were often a reclusive bunch, who kept to themselves, though where dying existed in the large towns of England and especially on the Continent of Europe, the guilds set up to protect the interests of dyers were some of the strongest and most political in the whole history of the guild system. As early as 1472, King Edward IV incorporated the Dyers Guild in London and it soon became a very powerful institution. It tended to serve the needs of the first league of dyers, who were producing the vibrant colours only rich people could afford, whilst country dyers remained isolated and insular.

It was quite definitely the introduction of better dyes, together with alum production in England that allowed the finished woollen textile trade to flourish in the way it did from Tudor times onward.

Dying required a significant supply of water close at hand. Some dyes only work when the cloth is boiled, so fuel was also an issue. Over the years new dyes gradually became available.[62] For example in 1766 a Dr Cuthbert Gordon of Glasgow, Scotland, discovered dyes that could be extracted from a range of lichens. He called his process and the dyes produced 'Cudbear' and patented his method of production. By 1774 Prussian Blue, a very popular colour, became available in Britain. This was one of the very early chemical dyes and was derived from prussite of potash and iron salts. An American from Massachusetts by the name of Dr Edward Bancroft discovered the use of quercitron bark and introduced it to dying in 1775. The bark gave a very bright yellow that soon became extremely popular.

As trade in textiles of all sorts began to gain ground and as the disposable income of individuals began to rise, so ever better and more colourfast dyes were avidly sought. New techniques in bleaching appeared, together with a better understanding of acids and alkalis and the way they worked in the dying trade. By 1834 a German-born scientist, Friedlieb Runge noticed that if he distilled coal tar, the alkaline released would give a bright blue colour if it was also treated with bleaching powder. Runge might rightfully be considered the father of alkaline dyes but the real innovation in this area did not come until two decades later.

William Henry Perkin was born in London in 1838.[63] A very bright child, and always keen to follow a career in chemistry, William entered the City of London School at the age of 15 and in 1853 was enrolled at the Royal College of Chemistry. His work on a possible cure for malaria accidentally led him to one of the most important discoveries textiles would ever know. Perkin was working at home, trying to establish a way to produce quinine artificially. He tried many concoctions and it was while he was treating analine sulphate with bichromate of potash that he made an unexpected breakthrough in dye production. What resulted was a black residue,

62 *Dyes: From Sea Snails to Synthetics*, Ruth G Kassinger, Twenty-First Century Books, 2003

63 *"The centenary of a great discovery: Sir William Henry Perkin's mauve"*, *Manchester Guardian*, 1956

analine black, from which Perkin eventually obtained a colourfast dye that was blue or mauve.[64] These were colours that were avidly sought for textiles and which had previously been difficult and somewhat expensive to produce.

Perkin, together with his family, opened a dye works in Harrow. There he worked for some years on a range of different dyes obtained from coal tar, before making his fortune and committing the rest of his life to pure chemical research.

Over the years one colour followed another, feeding an ever-growing demand from the public for a range of vibrant colours that could never have been created from natural dyes. In 1858 François-Emmanuel Verguin discovered magenta. This was the second of the anoline dyes and became more widely used than mauve. Safranine T, Lauth perfected violet in 1861 and then a German scientist, August Wilhelm von Hofmann, introduced another violet. Hofmann was one of the greatest dye chemists of all time. Working extensively with benzine, he learned more about the properties of anoline dyes than had previously been known and helped to spur on further discoveries. By 1868, two more German chemists, Graebe and Liebermann produced a substance known as 'alizarin' which was a chemical substitute for madder – the first time that a chemical dye had replaced such an established plant dye.

A whole range of deep blues, vibrant reds, greens and indigos followed, eventually allowing chemists in the textile trade to be very specific about the way colours would turn out in finished cloth. In more and more cases woollen yarn was dyed before it was woven, allowing an infinite combination of colours to be created in the finished cloth. Dyes were also created that proved ideal for printing onto material such as calico.

As for alum, the substance that allowed brightly coloured woollen cloth to be made in England, right back to the days of Good Queen Bess, it is still produced in Britain in large quantities. Alum is now derived from blast furnace slags, clays and other alumino-silicates

---

64 *Mauve: How One Man Invented a Colour That Changed the World*, Simon Garfield, Faber and Faber, 2001

and by processes that are far less time-dependent than those used on the Yorkshire coast for so long. New sorts of mordents are also available, together with a range of synthetic dyes that readily 'fix' to cloth and which do not fade over time or with washing. The evolution of such dyes during the 19th century greatly assisted the European and US chemical industries at a crucial stage in their development, bringing much needed capital to a branch of science to which we all owe a great debt in every facet of our daily lives.

The world turns pink

By the middle of the 19th century the Industrial Revolution in Britain was in full swing. On the Continent of Europe, only Belgium had begun a process towards industrialisation at anything like the same time it had taken place in Britain. Belgium began to take its first steps around 1830 whilst France, though it was one of the largest countries in Europe, took significantly longer to join the technological race. Some attempt had been made as early as 1784, when Gabriel Jars, a member of the French Academy of Sciences, had tried to transfer the methods of iron making in Britain to the Burgundy region of France. His efforts largely failed and there are several reasons why Le Creusot, as the ironworks were called, did not meet with immediate success.

France, like much of Europe, had been enmeshed in wars of one sort or another almost constantly since at least 1792. This had led to massive instability and did not provide the right social or financial circumstances for industrialisation to take place. Le Creusot failed partly because of this but also on account of the inability of Gabriel Jars to find the workforce he needed to run his ironworks. When workers were brought in from outside, they were generally disliked and mistrusted by the French, whilst locals were tied to the land and were unwilling to abandon a way of life they had known for countless generations. This was a direct reversal of what had happened as early as the 13th century when the Cistercian monks had made this part of France the very centre of European iron production.

It was a whole raft of circumstances that not only allowed Britain to take the initiative with industrialisation but also to acquire the biggest empire the world had ever known. Most of these circumstances were inextricably tied to sheep and their wool.

The mass exodus from the countryside in Britain, brought about primarily because of land enclosure, provided a ready-made workforce that was happy to obtain work and therefore the means of sustenance in any way possible. Britain had also gained a prosperous middle class. This gradually began to emerge after the Reformation, creating a social structure quite different than anything to be seen on the Continent at the time. The landed middle-class, unlike the aristocracy of old, was not only willing but determined to make money from its possessions and this of course included the vast acres prosperous families had acquired. The relative consistency and stability of the textile trade, even well before industrialisation, promised a ready profit for anyone keeping significant herds of sheep. At the same time arable farming was improving greatly, allowing profit to be made by growing wheat and barley in order to sustain a rapidly rising population that had no way to procure food in any other way but through purchase.

Being a series of Islands, Great Britain had managed to retain a degree of social stability that had been quite impossible across most of Europe. Britain fought many wars over the centuries, but it was never successfully conquered by another nation after the Norman Conquest of 1066. As a result it had prosecuted many of its wars on other people's soil. Even when royal dynasties had changed, causing civil strife within Britain itself, there had been little change within the basic structures that were in place. Although the English Civil War of the 17th century had stopped most of Britain in its tracks for a few years, the result was a more politically astute population that was not subject to the religious wars taking place elsewhere. The existence of a rising middle class was actually assisted by the Civil War, which in terms of Britain's ultimate prosperity probably turned out to be a good rather than a bad thing.

England, and then Britain as a whole, always seems to have been in the right place to capitalise when events turned ugly elsewhere and from an early time Britain possessed a strong navy that could defend its own shores, and enforce its policies abroad. The Napoleonic period, which might well have led to a united Europe that could have gained ground rapidly, actually resulted in a more fractional situation on the Continent than had existed previously. It also robbed France of its best in terms of money and manpower at exactly the same time industrialisation was beginning to take place in Britain. Napoleon's blockade of the Continent, which had been designed to starve Britain into submission, hit parts of Europe much harder than they did Britain herself because many European states simply could not function without the imports they had come to expect from across the Channel.

The blockade was difficult to maintain and in any case there were certain commodities that even Napoleon could not get in the quantities he required anywhere else but Britain. A good example of this was boots for his Grand Army. When Napoleon decided to invade Russia in 1812, he was forced to buy one million pairs of boots from Northampton, which flourished and grew as a result of the order. Meanwhile the early textile mills of West Yorkshire and elsewhere were working as hard as they could to supply woollen cloth that not only went to the manufacture of greatcoats for British soldiers, but also for their French counterparts and for the Russians too.

The subject of the British Empire rarely comes up in polite conversation within Britain these days. It is as if most people are either consciously or subconsciously ashamed of the historical period during which these small islands controlled such a large part of the Earth. This is quite understandable in terms of 21st century values. There is nothing heroic or morally justifiable about subjugating millions of people in lands far from one's own shores. The sort of racism inherent in an Empire such as that possessed by Britain is frowned upon in a modern Europe, the ethos of which is based squarely on equality of opportunity and personal freedom.

Despite modern sensibilities the British Empire did exist and it played a fantastically important part in the development of the world we live in today. Gathering together an empire meant that

Britain had a captive market for its products. Losing North America in the 18th century was something of a setback but it was more than compensated for by colonies in Africa, India, the Near East, Middle East, Far East, in the Southern Hemisphere and in Canada. At a time when Europe was in an almost constant state of ferment, Britain turned her attention to the world as a whole and so avoided many of the problems.

By the year 1812, the same year Napoleon invaded Russia, cotton textiles were already beginning to overtake wool as Britain's chief export. Much of the British Empire existed in climates far warmer than that to be found within the British Isles and it was predominantly to the export trade that most of the finished cotton cloth was bound. By the year 1830 more than a staggering 50% of the value of Britain's home produced exports came from the trade in cotton cloth. Wool, even at the height of its power, had never reached any more than 25% to 30%. Areas such as the English Midlands and the Clyde region of Scotland, where cotton had once had a foothold, were soon driven out of business by the sheer power of the cotton barons of Lancashire. Even in 1812 there were 250,000 weavers and 100,000 spinners creating the cotton textiles that the British merchant fleet was taking all over the globe.

Meanwhile, former rivals of Britain in the quest for empire building had fallen far behind. Spain, which had shown so much promise, both as a wool exporter and in terms of its overseas possessions, managed to destroy itself quite early. In particular the policies of King Philip II, who reigned from 1556 – 1598, sowed the seeds of his country's eventual downfall. He fought too many wars, failed to realise the significance of the rise of Protestantism, bled his colonies dry and thought little about the welfare of his people. Spain was already in decline by the middle of the 17th century and its position as a great exporter of wool was dented by the fact that its vulnerable pastures were overgrazed.

Another major competitor of Britain was Portugal, a nation that also shot itself in the foot in a number of different ways. Its decline partly matched that of its larger neighbour Spain but also came about because the Portuguese failed to people their overseas territories with colonists from their own country. Rather they constantly sent out bands of men whose chief aim was to draw as much money from the colonies as possible. With no women around of their own nationality these men invariably married locals and the Portuguese colonies began to take on their own character. At the time of the Napoleonic era the Portuguese royal family sailed to Brazil and did not return until Napoleon was overthrown. Portugal underwent a long period of social and economic instability that meant it eventually became nothing more than a shadow of what it had once been.

The third power that rivalled Britain for a long time was Holland. The Dutch maintained a large merchant and fighting fleet and in the early years of North American colonisation had beaten Britain to the punch every time. The chief problems for the Dutch had been two wars; the Nine Years War from 1688-1697 and the War of the Spanish Succession that lasted between 1702 and 1713. Both had brought great instability to the Dutch in their own lands and had prevented capital passing to overseas mercantile ventures.

Britain's main opponent from earliest times was her nearest neighbour across the English Channel. France continued to be a major threat until the early years of the 19th century. But France too had its own problems. In particular these had a bearing on its navy. During the French Revolution at the end of the 18th century and the beginning of the 19th, countless French aristocrats had been executed. Some of these had been leading admirals and captains in the navy. In those years during which Napoleon was dominating Europe, the absence of good commanders for his fighting ships made the force vulnerable to a more stable and professional British navy. In a series of pitched battles, such as that of Trafalgar in 1805, a large proportion of the French warships were destroyed. France also lost ground because of Napoleon's disastrous invasion of Russia in 1812 and on account of the seesawing between monarchy and republic that followed Napoleon's downfall.

As early as 1740 a poem by James Thomson was put to music by Thomas Augustine. It was to become a song dear to the heart of the British and is still sung on national occasions. The first line goes:

'Rule Britannia, Britannia rules the waves...'

This was no idle boast. Partly as a result of able management but mostly on account of incredible good luck, there was not a fighting force in the world that could stand up to that of Britain by the beginning of the 19th century, and especially not at sea. The result was the largest empire the world has ever known.[65] It eventually contained between 500 – 600 million people (at a time when the population of Britain was only 8 million) and covered 15.1 million square miles (37 million square kilometres). At its height the British Empire accounted for at least 35% of the total land area of the Earth.

The existence of such an empire, whether we applaud its reality or not these days, is all the more incredible when it is realised just how small the British Isles is. Historical maps show great swathes of pink across the globe, the colour denoting the British Empire. They bring home forcefully how remarkable the journey from isolated islands to the world's number one nation had been.

Not that the existence of such a huge and profitable empire had any great bearing on the lives of ordinary people within Britain itself. It is often suggested that at the time of the abolition of slavery, which was passed by act of Parliament in Britain in 1833, literally millions of people in Britain were living lives that were just as bad, if not worse, than the slaves themselves.

Terrible working and living conditions existed for people in many trades. Prior to 1819 there was absolutely no legislation regarding child labour. In woollen and cotton mills it was quite customary for children as young as 4 or 5 years to work a 12-hour day. Such young children were too small to supervise the machinery but were useful in other ways. Very small children often spent their days in amongst the machinery in spinning mills. Threads sometimes became detached and had to be 'picked out' when they fell to the floor. The small bodies and tiny hands of little children made them ideal for

---

65 *Empire: How Britain Made the Modern World*, Niall Furguson, Penguin Books, 2004
The Rise and Fall of the British Empire, Lawrence James, Abacus, 1995

this task but it will never be known how many were maimed or killed by mechanical components and drive belts.

In a typical woollen or cotton mill the day began early and finished late. The owner of a cotton mill in 1836 complained bitterly at the way Parliament kept legislating about the hours his mill-hands were allowed to work in any given week. He thought himself one of the most liberal of employers saying *'We never worked more than seventy-one hours a week before Sir John Hobhouse's Act was passed!'* He went on to say: *'We then came down to sixty-nine hours and since Lord Althorpe's Act was passed in 1833, we have reduced the hours to sixty-seven and a half hours for adults and that of children under thirteen years to forty-eight hours a week.'*

It was reported to a Parliamentary enquiry in 1879 that thirteen-hour days, with only fifteen minutes break, were still not uncommon. Wages were extremely low, forcing families to take their children with them to the mills, simply to try and make ends meet. For most, schooling was out of the question. The usual food of mill workers in the North of England was 'stirabout'. This was made from oatmeal, sometimes fried with a little dripping if any could be afforded. If meat was eaten at all it was only on the occasional holiday. Living conditions for workers in many trades were abysmal. Whole families in the cities lived in one-up-and-one-down terraced houses, invariably with toilet facilities that were shared by a number of dwellings and even these being only earth-closets. The Victorian novelist Charles Dickens, who often described the dirt and squalor of London in his books, nevertheless described Leeds as *'the filthiest and most awful place I have ever seen.'*

In Farsely, the village near Leeds where the first Australian wool had been sent at the beginning of the 19th century, there was a district known as Bagley – the place where Samuel Marsden had been born. Down a long lane from Farsley to Bagley, tiny houses were squeezed onto the road front, with a stream running down the back of the properties. Water for drinking was drawn from the stream, but the 'privies' often leaked into it. As a result typhoid and cholera were prevalent and of course they took the weakest of Farsley's population – the young and the old. The average life expectancy in the healthier parts of Britain was around 45 years, but in the mill towns of the North, with Farsley as a typical example, it was often as low as 26 years. In Bradford, where over 200 chimneys constantly rained pollution down on the town, and where water and sewage also shared the same stream, life expectancy in early Victorian times was a pitiful 18 years.

Industrial injuries were common, and not just to children. Advances in the design of spinning machines and looms saw them running at ever-greater speeds. There is one Yorkshire folk song from the period that is entitled 'Poverty Knocks'. It was sung in time to the sound of the machinery. One of the verses goes:

'Sometimes a shuttle flies out, and gives some poor woman a clout.
As she lies there bleeding there's no one a heeding
For who's there to carry her out?'

In addition to the machinery itself workers were subjected to the dangers from belting and pulleys. With most mills run by one or two large steam engines, power to drive individual machines had to somehow be transferred to the weaving shed. This was achieved by way of gear wheels and shafts. Shafts ran across the weaving shed above the heads of workers, but their power was passed to individual spinning machines and looms by way of thick belts which turned at a fast pace. Anyone whose clothing, hair or limbs became trapped between one of these belts and the pulleys around which it ran could expect to be badly injured, or killed.

Respiratory ailments were also common in mills, mainly because of the airborn fibres created during the spinning and weaving process. This was particularly true in the case of cotton mills, where over the decades thousands of people had their lives significantly shortened.

Anyone visiting one of the small recreated textile mills housed in the Industrial Museums of Yorkshire or Lancashire these days is always stunned by the sheer volume of noise created by the machinery. Deafness in middle age was almost universal and workers in the textile trade soon learned to be excellent lip-readers because it was the only way they could communicate.

Wool and cotton built an Empire and made mill owners into millionaires but it did nothing to improve the lot of ordinary workers. It says something about either the character or the forbearance of the British mentality that the result was not a full-scale revolution.

Fortunately it eventually dawned on at least some mill owners that it was not in their best interests to have their workers dead or maimed before they had even reached their early middle years. The efforts of a few far-sighted individuals to improve the lot of the men, women and children of the mills has often been referred to as philanthropy but in many cases it was a matter of plain self-interest. But whatever the motives, these forward-looking employers did begin to improve matters for those upon whom they relied.

A good example is that of Titus Salt.[66] He was the son of a woolstapler from Morley near Leeds and after completing his education he joined the family firm in 1824. In 1833 Titus took over the running of the expanding business and eventually became the biggest employer in Bradford, by this time owning a number of different mills.

Titus Salt began to realise that the terrible pollution in Bradford was shortening the life of everyone living there and he experimented with ways to cut down on sulphur emission from the factory chimneys. Although he was successful, other employers in the town were unwilling to spend the money necessary to make the improvements. Salt decided to move his entire production base out of Bradford and eventually settled on a spot at Shipley, near the River Aire and the Leeds and Liverpool Canal, just a few miles from Bradford. With characteristic Victorian modesty he named his new factory and township 'Saltaire', a composite of his own name and that of the river.

When the Saltaire factory first opened in the early 1850s Salt's 3,500 workers travelled on a daily basis from Bradford but this state of affairs was far from ideal. He commenced a large building scheme that resulted in 850 well-appointed houses, with a school,

---

66 *The Great Paternalist: Titus Salt and the Growth of Nineteenth-Century Bradford*, Jack Reynolds, M Temple Smith, 1983

chapels and a hospital. Although a confirmed authoritarian (for example he would survey his domains from the tower of his chapel every Sunday and physically cut down any washing lines he saw in use) Titus Salt did have more of a social conscience than most mill owners of his day. He opposed child labour, cut down hours of work and supported reforms of factories generally. Nevertheless, he always had one eye on his business.

The mill at Saltaire had 14 boilers that supplied steam to four massive steam engines. These powered 1,200 looms in one of the biggest weaving sheds ever created. At its peak the factory turned out 30,000 yards (17 miles) of cloth six days a week. Salt was a worsted manufacture, creating cloth from long-staple wool, but as time went by he also diversified into cloth that was a mixture of cotton and the very fine wool of the Alpaca. Experiments in rearing Alpaca in Yorkshire were undertaken by Salt, making the hills around the Aire Valley reminiscent of the lower slopes of the Andes.

By the end of the 19th century many other countries of the world were beginning to catch up with the lead Britain had gained in terms of her technological development and her industrialisation. This was especially true of Germany, which began to gain ground quickly in the 1880s and 1890s, mainly thanks to its excellent reserves of coal and iron. The US was also moving forward rapidly with new territories being opened up and the industrial base of the country gaining pace. The race for Empire was still on and there was a particular rivalry between Germany, which had come late to the party of parcelling up parts of the world, and Britain, whose empire was all but complete by the end of the 19th century.

Although woollen cloth played a significant but not critical part in Britain's exports by the beginning of the 20th century, it still had the power to cause major world events, or at least to contribute significantly to them. A good example was 'Springfield Mill', owned by Rubin Gaunt and company and situated in that same village of Farsley we have visited several times already. The First World War saw the eventual redrawing of the map of Europe. It brought millions of armed men to battle from dozens of different nations. One of these was Russia, which at the outbreak of the war was fighting for the allies against Germany.

History relates that in November 1917 the Bolsheviks under Lenin gained possession of Moscow, which heralded a general revolution in Russia. This ultimately set the seal on the next sixty years of Russian history, during which time it fell under communist rule and was known as the USSR. However, the revolution did not come out of thin air. Unrest in Russia had been mounting for a long time but what really allowed the Bolsheviks to seize power was the disastrous prosecution of the First World War by the Russian Tsar and his generals. By 1916 the Russians were faring badly on all fronts, though in many places they were holding their own against the German forces. What really swung the balance was a lack of equipment, and in particular that of uniforms for the ordinary soldiers. This situation came about partly as a result of Britain's own war effort taking place at the same time.

Before the start of the war the mills of the West Riding, and those of Farsley in particular, had been working flat out to provide the woollen cloth necessary for army greatcoats – as indeed had been the case for earlier conflicts right back to the Napoleonic Wars. An information book for Springbank Mill, written when it was still trading as a woollen mill, notes that the factory had a big part to play in causing the Russian revolution, through no real fault of anyone managing or working in the mill.

Countless thousands of soldiers from Britain and the armies of her Empire and dependencies were being shipped to France, there to fight the Germans on the Western Front. All of these soldiers also required uniforms and the government of Britain gave instructions that mills such as Springbank Mill were to switch production to making the cloth needed for the British Army.

This meant that there was no production capacity left to continue supplying the Russian army with the cloth it needed. The Bolsheviks in both Moscow and St Petersburg relied heavily for support on soldiers who mutinied from the army and returned to fight as revolutionaries in the cities. One of the main reasons why the Russian soldiers had thrown down their weapons was not as a result of their revolutionary fervour, but rather because their clothes and boots had fallen to pieces and that no new uniforms were forthcoming. Trying to survive in the harsh weather conditions of the Russian front was impossible without warm clothing and so the soldiers eventually simply turned around and marched home. Springbank Mill may not have directly caused the Russian revolution, but its inability, together with that of other woollen mills, to make enough cloth for both Russia and the home forces certainly made a bad situation worse.

After the First World War, Britain gradually began to lose the hold she had enjoyed within the wider world. Other countries started to build huge navies and the strain of trying to police and govern such a large empire began to tell. Whereas Britain had enjoyed a monopoly in manufacturing prior to the 1920's and 1930's, other countries were soon snapping at her heels. This does not detract from the fact that the British legacy was massive. There are presently around 341 million people in the world who count English as their native tongue. This number is beaten only by Mandarin Chinese and Hindi in India, though this situation only comes about because of the massive home populations of China and India.

English is far better spread across the world than any other language. It is the official language of 52 countries, together with numerous other small states and dependencies. Between ¼ and 1/3 of the entire population of the world understand and can speak English, which is the established tongue of diplomacy and technology. In 2001, 189 countries of the United Nations were asked what language they wished to use to communicate with embassies in other countries. 120 of those asked stated that they would wish to use English. Only 40 cited French and 20 wished to use Spanish.

This state of affairs is undoubtedly a legacy of the British Empire, together with the fact that the United States, which developed out of what was once also a British colony, is now so influential in the world as a whole. The fate of the world as we know it today would have been very different if the British Empire had not existed and there can be no doubt that the circumstances that saw the creation of the Empire were primarily due to historical forces at work in Britain for many centuries. First amongst these was an ability to sustain significant exports and thereby to build a solid economy. It cannot be denied that Britain's position as a series of islands, removed from much of the fighting that constantly took place in Europe, was a significant factor but this is far from being the whole story. After all, Europe has many islands but none of them developed in the way Britain did.

From first to last the specific factor that allowed Britain to develop in the way she did was the presence of large flocks of sheep. In an unbroken history that goes back at least as far as Roman times, the islands that comprise Britain proved ideal for the breeding of sheep with good quality fleeces. The wool produced sustained the economies of countries far from Britain's own shores but when these places went through problems of their own, Britain was able to switch from raw wool production to finished textiles. The expertise that already existed in the North of England in the handling of textiles made the area ideal for the creation of cotton cloth and good contacts with the world made it possible to obtain the raw material.

Within Britain itself, there are many areas that claim to have been pivotal to and even responsible for the massive Industrial revolution of the 18th and 19th centuries. Industrialisation could not have taken place without the metal workers of Birmingham or the steel kings of Sheffield and eventually Middlesborough. The coalfields of many parts of Britain kept people warm and fuelled the new steam engines that drove industrialisation. Farmers learned new agricultural techniques that allowed them to feed a rapidly growing population and fishermen all around the coasts braved rough seas to bring home catches that were also vital.

Once unleashed, the Industrial revolution was an unstoppable leviathan but the best evidence we have for what really brought it about comes from Daniel Defoe, the man who travelled through the whole of Britain at probably the most pivotal time in its history. He was in no doubt whatsoever that Britain was a place built on sheep. The nucleus of other industries were evident to him but he paid them scant attention, concentrating instead on the massive herds of sheep in so many parts of the Islands and the tremendous capacity of textile production, even though it was still being carried out as a cottage industry.

History is a matter of consequences – often ones over which individuals and even nations have little control. The Victorians may have believed that Britain had been singled out by an interested deity to stand as a paragon of virtue and industry but they saw only the end product of centuries of serendipity. There were and are in the world dozens of examples of cultures that predated Britain by thousands of years. The Egyptians, Babylonians, Greeks, Romans, Persians, Indians, Chinese and many other races added to the rise of humanity and offered models for civilization. Some of these cultures spanned thousands of years. Great Britain learned something important from all these peoples and its own greatness was little more than a brief spark in the darkness of history. The tinder that allowed that spark to burst into flame in the 21st century was wool and the wealth it offered. This is particularly evident in terms of the rise of capitalism, the economic system upon which all of Western Democracy is based.

Credit where credit's due

There was a time in which the only reliable way to trade was through barter. You had a cabbage that I wanted, and I had a leather purse you needed. If I thought your cabbage was worth about as much as my purse, we would simply swap. However, I might think the purse was worth more and demand two cabbages for it and eventually a deal would be struck.

Developing societies soon began to use coinage instead of barter – simply because it was more convenient. Precious metals, such as gold and silver, were stamped out into known weights. Sometimes the coins were created by regions or institutions, but increasingly, at least from Roman times onwards, they were issued by the state. Now if I wanted your cabbage I would have to swap it for a coin. You wouldn't have the cabbage any more but you could take the coin to someone else, for example a person who had made a pair of shoes that took your fancy.

Despite the fact that coins were originally made from precious metals, there was still a degree of trust involved, which is not the case with barter. Those using coinage trusted that the coins were genuine and that they contained the prescribed amount of precious metal. They also maintained a trust in the 'buying power' of a given coin – after all, if everyone suddenly decided that silver and gold were fairly useless metals and of no value whatsoever, you would have been better off keeping your cabbage – at least you could eat it!

In principle though, coinage was fairly reliable. The amount of gold or silver in circulation at any point in time was limited and in any given country it represented that state's overall assets and therefore people possessing coins had a stake in the wealth of their country. Coins maintained a genuine value because everyone agreed that gold and silver were precious. The same is not true of paper money, which had no intrinsic value whatsoever. The words printed on every British bank note bear out the fact that what we are actually spending has no worth it its own right.

'I promise to pay the bearer on demand the sum of ...'

The difference between coins and paper money lies in the fact that the bank note merely 'represents' a certain amount of gold that is theoretically held in a bank somewhere. In principle, if there are 1,000,000 bank notes in circulation in the US, and if each note has a face value of $1, there ought to be $1,000,000 worth of gold sitting in some secure vault to cover the promissory value of the notes. Originally this may sometimes have been the case, but it is far from being the truth of the matter now.

Paper money developed in the Middle Ages, and for a very important reason. Personal security left a lot to be desired and keeping a whole stack of gold coins in one's house, or worse still about one's person, was risky. There were thieves and cut-purses everywhere, just waiting to divest anyone foolish enough to be off their guard of their hard earned money.

As a result people across Europe took to depositing their spare coinage in the much safer premises of someone such as a goldsmith. Since he was working all the time with precious metals the goldsmith took significant precautions against theft. He might be the only person in a town with sufficient need, and enough wealth, to purchase strongboxes or early forms of safe. Of course the goldsmith would charge a small amount for the service he was offering and he would give anyone depositing money with him a receipt. Over time it dawned on people that, in principle, their receipts were worth the same as the value of the coins they detailed. It therefore became useful to undertake transactions without having to remove money from the goldsmith's shop, but rather to simply transfer a receipt from one person to another.

Somewhere along the line it occurred to a goldsmith that he had many hundreds of gold and silver coins sitting in his vault, doing absolutely nothing. The chances of everyone in his community demanding their coins back on the same day, or even the same year, were extremely small. Would it therefore not be useful to somehow 'invest' the coins in some venture that would make a profit? It gradually became recognised that only around 10% of the true value of receipts in circulation needed to be covered by actual coinage without the goldsmith needing to worry too much.

So now our enterprising goldsmith 'lent' some of the money from his vault to an individual who was willing to pay him back across a prescribed period, together with interest. This was a bit of a problem in Christian countries because the charging of interest, known as usury, was contrary to Christian law. Fortunately, many of the goldsmith's of Medieval Europe were not Christians, they were Jews. Judaism had no taboo about usury, except when dealing with others of the Jewish persuasion, and so the system worked fairly well.

Banks came into being when those depositing money were aware of what the goldsmith was doing with their cash and, probably reasonably, demanded a share of the profit he was making through lending out 'their' money. As a result a decision was taken to pay the investor a part of the interest the goldsmith was getting from his borrowers. This was fairer than simply using other people's money without their consent and the investor was aware that there was a degree of 'risk' involved if borrowers did not repay loans that had been advanced to them.

Banks grew and flourished, eventually run by all manner of people and not simply goldsmiths. Governments eventually began to form National Banks, such as the Bank of England, created in 1694 by a group of far-sighted wealthy businessmen, responding not to an individual but a government anxious to borrow money. The amount they lent became known as the National Debt, the interest on which was repaid by the government from the taxes it imposed on the populace of England. Bank notes were issued by the government, quite soon covering amounts that could not be redeemed by handing the note over a counter in exchange for real gold – simply because there was not enough gold in any bank to cover the value of the notes. This doesn't really matter as long as everyone involved in the system 'trusts' it. Most of us no longer relate our bank notes to gold at all. We see the notes as having genuine value in their own right.

Anyone wanting a loan, from either the goldsmith or the embryonic bank, would most likely have to offer some sort of security against default on the repayment – for example the deeds to his farm or house. In that respect things haven't changed too much. Eventually, and particularly by the start of the Industrial Revolution, people began to borrow large amounts of money from the newly formed banking institutions, and also from rich investors, to cover the cost of opening factories and mills. The return on money lent in this way could be significant so many of those who had money saw the risk as worthwhile.

It wasn't too long before the notion of sharing the risk took another turn. Shares were invented, especially for large projects like railways, and people could part with a little of their money in order to own a stake in the enterprise. In return for their money they would be issued with a share certificate. If the railroad did well, the shares increased in value on the open market, simply because people generally 'considered' them to be more valuable. Shareholders could also receive dividends if the enterprise proved profitable. Specific places developed where people would go to buy and sell shares and so stock markets were born. There were setbacks, like the infamous South Sea Bubble scam in 18th-century Britain, when thousands of shares were sold relating to something that didn't really exist at all, but in the main the system worked very well.

Over a long period of time, governments interfered less and less in 'how' money was being made. They allowed markets to find their own value and accepted that, generally speaking, business ventures were the prerogative of individuals, whilst running the country was the government's concern. This separation of national authority and private business lies at the heart of Capitalism, the economic system by which most democratic Western countries are presently run.

Some experts would disagree that most of us now live in truly Capitalist societies, pointing out that governments do interfere with the basic economic structures these days. They suggest that in countries like the US and Britain what really exists is a 'mixed economy', in which Capitalism represents only one part of the overall economic system.

Capitalism is a complicated business and sometimes it all goes terribly wrong. In the 1930s for a whole variety of reasons, investors suddenly lost their trust in shares and what followed was known as the Depression. Previously wealthy companies suddenly became virtually worthless – though the only thing that had changed was how much confidence individuals had in them. Millions of people across the Western world and beyond were suddenly thrown out of work and became impoverished as a result. Advocates of other economic models, such as Fascism and Communism, pointed to events like the depression, considering that it was not right that a relatively few rich individuals should be able to bring whole nations to their knees by speculating. Nevertheless, the markets recovered and despite its flaws Capitalism has outlived other economic models from the recent past. It might not be the best system imaginable but it does seem to work fairly well.

If it had not been for the willingness of individuals to take risks with their money, industrialisation could never have taken place. There were some projects, for example canals, railways, gas and electric supply, the building of vast dams and reservoirs and the like, that would have been too expensive for any one individual to undertake.

We can see the gradual building of Capitalism from the 18th century on but the mechanisms that allowed it to flourish and grow were already in place. Where did they originate? Was it all simply an extension of those first coins left in the goldsmith's shop? There is at least one example from history of an influential group of people who, from a very early period, sowed the seeds of the modern world by taking steps that, at the time, were quite revolutionary.

It was back in the 12th century that one very important group of people had the bright idea to use receipts in a different way to that employed by the local goldsmith. Let us suppose that a merchant from London wanted to travel to Paris, there to purchase pepper that he could bring back and sell at a profit in London. Individual receipts might work very well in the streets of his own city but Paris was many miles away, and in a different country altogether. The receipt from a London goldsmith would be worth nothing on the other side of the English Channel. This meant that the merchant had little choice but to carry the necessary cash with him, in the form of gold or silver coins. Not only was this risky, it could be expensive. At the very least he would have to hire armed men to accompany him, which would much reduce his possible profit.

What was needed was an international version of the local goldsmith and this service was first provided by the Knights Templar. After its formation during the 12th century, the order of the Knights Templar spread across Western Europe, the Near and Middle East very quickly. The stated reason for the existence of the Templars was to fight alongside the Christian Crusaders, against the forces of Islam, especially in the Holy Land. This is exactly what they did, with great effectiveness and significant bravery. But fighting Muslims may not have been the only reason for the existence of the Templars.

During the research for two previous books, *The Goddess, the Grail and the Lodge*[67] and *The Virgin and the Pentacle*[68], I looked carefully at what was happening in France, and in particular a part of it known as Champagne, around the time the Templars were formed. As I pointed out in Chapter 5, the Knights Templar soon expanded their range of interests, becoming merchant shippers and bankers in their own right. It was they who were first able to address the problem of the merchant from London outlined above. What happened is that the merchant would take a walk down to an area of London off Fleet Street, which even to this day is known as 'The Temple'. There he would come across the London headquarters of the Knights Templars.

67   *The Goddess, the Grail and the Lodge*, Alan Butler, O Books, 2004
68   *The Virgin and the Pentacle*, Alan Butler, O Books, 2005

Our merchant would deposit his gold with the Templars and they would provide him with a receipt, which also carried a secret cipher that was understood only by the Templars themselves. Taking the note with him, the merchant would travel to Paris, where he would go directly to the Paris headquarters of the Templars. There he would hand over the note and receive in return the amount of money he had deposited in London, in local currency. It was an invaluable service and if our merchant wasn't the brightest person in the world he might even think the whole undertaking was completely free of charge.

The Templars must have been very much aware that Christianity forbade the charging of interest. With time they would simply ignore this fact because the only authority that could take action against them was the Pope, for whom they were eventually earning large amounts of money. This was because in many countries the Templars collected church tithes. Everyone in countries across the Christian world was supposed to give 10% of all they earned to the Church and a fair slice of this eventually found its way to the Vatican, thanks to the diligence of the Templar tax collectors. The Pope needed the Templars and wasn't about to do anything to kill a goose that was laying so many golden eggs. However, in the early days the Templars made their money on transactions such as the one outlined above by manipulating the 'exchange rate' between different currencies. Banks and other institutions that claim to exchange currencies for free these days are doing the same thing. They simply 'set' the exchange rate so that customers are not really getting full value for their money. In the days of the Templars this policy was hard to prove and could not really be called usury.

I also indicated in Chapter 5 that there is significant evidence that the Templars were created for quite specific reasons associated with the region known as Champagne. Champagne is in North Central France. During the 12th century the region was a 'duchy'. This meant it owed an allegiance to France itself, which in those distant days was very much smaller than it is now. Despite owing fealty to France, the Counts of Champagne did everything they could to remain as independent as possible and relations between the rulers of Champagne and the French kings were not always cordial.

At exactly the same time as the Templars were becoming a reality across Europe and beyond, moves were being made in Champagne to build a series of very important markets with quite specific intentions. Champagne is situated south of Paris, with its capital being the city of Troyes. Ever since Roman times special events known as 'fairs' had taken place in Champagne. Fairs were like markets, in that people came there to buy and sell merchandise, but whilst a market might be held every week, a fair only took place at very specific times of the year, usually associated with the feast day of a particular saint. This came about primarily because festivals were held on some saint's days. People would gather to celebrate, and whilst they were together, it also made sense to trade. Although the Champagne fairs were already old in the 12th century, there was nothing particularly special about them, until the reign of Count Thibaud II, who ruled in champagne between 1125 and 1151.

The previous Count of Champagne, Hughes, voluntarily surrendered his title in 1125, in order to go out to Jerusalem, there to join the first Templar knights, who had been living on the Temple mound by the King of Jerusalem's palace for over a decade. When his direct relative Thibaud began to rule Champagne he took very definite and quite immediate steps that simply cannot be unrelated to both the existence of the Cistercian order of monks and to that of the Templars. Thibaud revolutionised the existing fairs in Champagne, and increased their number. The fairs were spread around the towns of Champagne. Each year in January there was one at Lagny Sur Marne and on the last Tuesday before the middle of Lent there was another in Bar Sur Aube. In the month of May the fair of Provins took place and in August came that of Troyes. Provins had another fair in September and there was an additional fair in Troyes during October.

Although the Champagne fairs had historically dealt with a wealth of different merchandise and in fact continued to do so, Thibaud made changes that directly encouraged one specific group of people to attend in their hundreds. These were raw-wool and cloth merchants.

The real reason for the formation of strategic cloth fairs in the district was, in my opinion, part of a cohesive plan that also involved the creation of the Cistercian order and that of the Templars. We should not forget that the Templars had their origins and their main headquarters in Troyes, capital of Champagne, or that St Bernard of Clairvaux, by far and away the most important of the Cistercian leaders had his own abbey at Clairvaux, also in Champagne and very close to Troyes.

The Champagne fairs served the purposes of the Cistercians, the Templars and also the Counts of Champagne very well. Tons of wool was being produced in Cistercian monasteries, especially those in Britain. The vast majority of it was shipped directly to Flanders, where it was made into cloth. The Cistercians also had significant business interests in Flanders. It was they who had done the most to drain flooded land, to build dykes and to make much of Flanders into good farmland. The bulk of the cloth leaving Flanders during the 12th century was unfinished – in other words it was woven but not fulled or dyed. This cloth was brought down to the Champagne fairs, where it was traded with Italian merchants for commodities not readily available in north-western Europe, particularly luxury goods and spices from the East. The unfinished cloth was then taken to Italy, and in particular Florence, where it was dyed, fulled and finished, before being sold on the open market.

The Cistercians gained from the Champagne fairs because they found a ready market for their wool, by way of Flanders. At the same time Bernard of Clairvaux was offering assistance to his relatives in Champagne. Meanwhile the Templars, who became an official religious order in 1128, helped to supervise the fairs as well as acting as shippers and merchants and being wool producers in their own right. The fairs were taking place right on the doorstep of their own headquarters in Troyes and the original leaders of the Templars were from the same dynastic bloodlines as the Counts of Champagne and Bernard of Clairvaux. Finally the Counts of Champagne gained from the fairs both in terms of prestige and revenue. They guaranteed safe passage to all those taking part, supervised the buying and selling and collected significant taxes for their efforts. In addition, the stronger Champagne became, the less it was obliged to bend the knee to successive French monarchs.

This comfortable clique, that seems to have been completely missed by historians, had quite clearly been working from at least the beginning of the 12th century, and probably a good deal earlier, in order to put its plans into action. The presence of this very early self-help group cannot be ignored, simply because the Champagne fairs were such an important component part in the development of international trade in Europe and beyond.

It was at the Champagne fairs that some of the earliest credit transactions were undertaken. These were arranged not only by the Templars but also by Jewish bankers and, somewhat later, by the embryonic banks that were developing in Italy.

Credit was hugely important in the development of international trade and eventually the creation of Capitalism. It began to work at the Champagne fairs by way of promissory notes. These were issued at the fairs and they allowed a given merchant to take the goods he required without payment. The money would become due at the next Champagne fair, allowing the merchant to 'realise' his assets in the meantime. Over time a whole raft of different strategies were employed to help the fairs run more smoothly and equitably for all concerned. They became the very heart of trade in and to Western Europe and represented an inspirational model.

People in other parts of Western Europe looked at the developing Champagne fairs with avaricious eyes. By the later 14th century a new series of such fairs began in Lyon, France and even earlier examples existed in Paris. King Philip IV of France, 1268 – 1314) took a series of steps, for example destroying the Knights Templar, that would spell the beginning of the end of the Champagne fairs from the beginning of the 14th century but this didn't matter in the greater scheme of things because the idea of international fairs and credit transactions had become so popular.

All manner of strategies were employed to ensure that any interest charges regarding transactions at the fairs was somehow hidden, in order that merchants could not be accused of usury. Eventually, every possible commodity imaginable was traded by way of the fairs but there is no doubt that at the heart of all of them wool remained the base and most important trade object. Wool, even in its raw state, was virtually a currency in its own right. Bales of wool can be stored for years if necessary before they are used – a policy still employed at times by countries such as Australia. What is more, the Vatican's share of English tithes was actually paid in raw wool for some centuries. Wool was tangible and reliable; it rarely depreciated in value and if of good quality, as English wool was, it would always find a ready market.

At the same time as the Templars came to grief, at the start of the 14th century, Italian woollen merchants such as the Medici were beginning to grow in wealth. They were ready to supply the same sort of credit facilities and loans that were common in the Champagne fairs. It is upon these first international credit and banking transactions that Capitalism was eventually based.

Gradually, as wars ravaged specific regions, dealings in credit transactions and early shares shifted about Europe from one place to another. As early as the late 13th century, whilst the Templars still existed, a group of commodity traders in Bruges, Belgium, began to gather together on a regular basis in the house of a man who had the name Van der Bourse. Their meetings were eventually formalised and gained their own premises, which kept the name – the Bourse. The idea of a place where bankers and speculators could meet rapidly caught on in Flanders, and soon spread to other parts of Europe. By the 16th century the Bourse in Antwerp was particularly successful and efforts were made in England to counter its monopolies and to bring some of the profits from trade across the English Channel.

The English response to the Bourse of Antwerp was the Royal Exchange. This was a large building erected by Sir Thomas Gresham, one of Queen Elizabeth I's advisers and favourites. Gresham was a mercer, in other words a wool merchant, from a family of mercers in Norfolk. The Queen was particularly interested in the Royal Exchange. Like most monarchs of the time she was invariably short of money. As with everyone else she could only really remedy this situation by taking out loans – though in this case on a grand scale.

Formerly, she had to go cap in hand to the speculators and bankers of Antwerp, simply because institutions such as the Bourse were nonexistent in England. The loans were forthcoming in Antwerp but the interest was prohibitive, something that simply had to be remedied if the Queen were not to be effectively bankrupt.

After 1568 significant gains in gold in England, much of which originated in plundered Spanish treasure galleons, was minted as English coins and at the suggestion of Gresham was put into circulation, particularly amongst the merchants. This meant the Queen could begin to obtain loans from the embryonic English bankers, and at very much more preferential rates. By 1568, just as so much new gold coin was appearing in England, Sir Thomas Gresham opened the Royal Exchange, built on a prestige site in Central London. Here, for the first time, banking and trading could be formalised and the place soon began to buzz. This particular building was destroyed in the Great Fire of London of 1666 but another was soon rebuilt on the same site.

From the late 16th century on, London never looked back and quickly became the most important financial centre anywhere. It is stated that even today the City of London represents the richest square mile of earth on the planet. It was within the city that loans were raised to pay for new settlements in the US and for speculative voyages to previously unexplored parts of the world. London financiers made the British Empire possible, and profited greatly from its existence.

Gone are the abacus and the entry books of the merchants and bankers, to be replaced by computers and high speed internet access that allow trading in hundreds of commodities to take place across the world at lightning speed. But language remains and the crucial importance of wool to the earliest capitalist markets is enshrined in the word 'staple'. Today we think of staples as being the basic foodstuffs that keep us alive – such as grain products or even bread for example. However, the word is very old and only came to be used in this way from the 16th or 17th century. It appears in several forms from a very early date. The 'Staple' was that place or places where English wool could be sold to the Continent of Europe. For much of the time this was Calais, but it had also been Antwerp and a whole series of ports in England.

Staple might be derived from a middle low-German word, 'stapel' which means 'shop'. If so it had an early association with markets. What this does not tell us is why the strands of raw wool are also called 'the staple'. Did this come about as a result of the markets and fairs at which wool was such an important trade item, or did the markets and ports take their name from the wool? Unfortunately nobody can answer this particular question. What does remain a fact is that in addition to all the other associations wool has with the building of the modern world, the very economic systems on which it so crucially depends were also brought about in great part thanks to the existence of sheep.

Man's best friend?

On 5 July 1996 a female lamb was born in Midlothian, Scotland. There's nothing too remarkable about that – after all millions of lambs are born every year across Britain, and many millions more throughout the world. What made this particular infant sheep so important was the fact that, alone in the world at the time, it had no natural mother or father. The ewe was a Finn Dorset, born at the Rosslin Institute, and she represented the first higher mammal to be cloned.

Once introduced to the world in February 1997 Dolly the sheep filled the headlines of newspapers and became the lead story in broadcasts all over the planet. She had been created by removing the material from the mature egg of an adult ewe, which was replaced by the nucleus of an adult sheep's mammary cell. The result was given a tiny electric shock and then transplanted into the womb of a host ewe. In a genetic sense Dolly was an exact copy of the donor sheep. This was another first for sheep – or in fact for any higher mammal.

The Roslin Institute, where Dolly was created, is a centre for genetic research into domestic animals and the real reason for Dolly's existence was part of the search to create the perfect sheep, but it has greater ramifications than this simple endeavour. Dolly was the first example of a technique that may one day allow new organs to be 'grown' for people with kidney, liver or other organ disease and though there are many people who see shades of 'Frankenstein' in the whole business, the significance of this event cannot be overstated.

How far humanity has come since that Stone Age hunter, probably somewhere in Asia, captured a wild lamb and set out to make it into the world's first domestic sheep. And how strange it is that when humanity reached a crossroads at which it was able to manipulate the very building blocks of life, a sheep was the first creature to take a step that makes it the first offspring ever born without parents, since the dawn of time.

There are presently just over one billion sheep in the world, which represents one sheep for every six people. Put into perspective, and assuming an average sheep to be one metre in length from nose to tail, the world's sheep population would form a snout to tail line that would go around the world twenty-five times! Taken together with goats the number is nearer two billion, which outnumbers any other domestic species – even cattle. Despite the fact that woollen textile production has been hit hard by the creation of manmade fibres, such as nylon, rayon and the like, wool remains extremely important as a renewable and natural resource. The production of manmade fibres constantly depletes our store of oil and coal reserves and their production adds significantly to greenhouse gases and ultimately to global warming. The same is not true in the case of wool. Place a suitable sheep on the right piece of ground – which is just about any ground – and it will do what sheep have always done, it will grow wool, whilst at the same time improving the land with its own droppings. It won't have any harmful effect on the atmosphere and it represents a sustainable resource that offers a good cash crop every year.

Sheep also have other ecological benefits. They are now being used extensively in the US and Canada to graze large tracts of open land between stands of timber. Their presence ensures that undergrowth is kept down and that in the hot summer months, fires that start amongst the trees cannot spread across the breaks. Sheep are also being used in many parts of the world to keep down noxious weeds, our woolly friends having a natural immunity to many.

As far as their reputation for stupidity is concerned it turns out that sheep are not half so dumb as we have always assumed. Recent experiments have shown that sheep are really quite bright. They have the ability to recognise their shepherds and each other. Nor do sheep have a short attention span. It was proved that sheep could remember the faces of their shepherds and other sheep amongst whom they had lived for up to two years. Some sheep have also learned to roll across cattle grids on their backs and new measures may have to be taken in order to keep them penned in because it has also been shown that they can teach each other this naughty trick.

Sheep are heavily represented amongst livestock that are crucially important to developing countries. Their sheer versatility sets them apart. Sheep are tough, easy to manage and can offer much more than wool. Dairy produce obtained from sheep is increasing every year across the world and sheep's cheese in particular has never been so popular as it is right now.

Amongst the really big sheep-breeding nations of the world China comes at the top of the list and presently has around 139,200,000 animals. The old feudal economy of China has changed markedly since the advent of communism but sheep are every bit as important to this massive nation as they ever were. The Chinese are great producers of woollen textiles and despite the vast herds of sheep the country possesses, China is still the biggest net importer of raw wool, particularly from Australia. However, this represents a very small proportion of the 302,000 tonnes of wool that is annually shorn from sheep in China itself. New projects for sheep rearing are being tried and there is no indication that the Chinese are intended to scale down their efforts to substantially increase their herds. Although sheep rearing has fallen in some first world countries, China's flocks are increasing by around 3% each year.

Next on the list for numbers of sheep comes Australia. It presently has 98,000,000 sheep and produces 302,000 tonnes of raw wool each year. Australia has come a very long way since the first penal colonies were founded there in the 18th century. With a population of 20,300,000 Australia is a boom economy and represent one of the great success stories of the modern world. Although sheep production has been on the wane down under, mainly due to the fact that wool is not so much in demand as it once was, there seems to be a bounce-back in operation. Sales of Australian wool in 2001 were worth $3.9 billion to the economy. The reason Australia is now doing better from its wool sales lies in the fact that although the total number of sheep in the country has fallen, the demand for wool on the world market is still strong. With demand outstripping supply, the price rises.

Iran is third on the list of countries that have the greatest number of sheep. Throughout the nation there are 53,000,000 sheep, used both for mutton and for wool. Between them the states of the former Soviet Union have 51,900,000 sheep and behind them comes India with 42,000,000 head.

By far and away the most successful sheep-breeding nation, bearing in mind the size of its population, is New Zealand, which has 10 sheep for every human and enjoys flocks of a staggering 46,000,000 animals. New Zealand, though also gaining ground technologically and in other ways, remains dependent on its wool and mutton. Despite the fact that its flocks are significantly smaller than those of China or Australia, New Zealand remains the second biggest exporter of wool. It produces 200,000 tons of clean wool for export each year. Together with Australia it ploughs millions of dollars each year into wool-based research, producing ever new and revolutionary ways of using this natural substance, all of which help to cut down our reliance on manmade fibre.

Great Britain is still a massive sheep breeding area, despite the fact that sheep farmers generally have had a lean time over the last few years. Prices for lamb have been low recently but across the United Kingdom there are still 25,000,000 sheep. With a population of 59,600,000, the UK maintains a sheep to people ratio of one sheep for every 2.3 people. At present the vast majority of British wool, in fact around 70%, does not find its way into clothing. Rather it is made into luxurious carpets, where its hardwearing quality is best employed.

In addition to the feeling of luxury that wool brings, even to the modern world, innovation remains the name of the game. New techniques are being developed to make wool more comfortable and to improve its ability to maintain its shape when it is washed. A new process developed in the US and known as 'bio-polishing' uses enzymes to dissolve those stray bits of yarn that can cause some people a degree of irritation. The same process allows wool to be dyed at lower temperatures than has traditionally been the case, causing less damage to the fibres. An unexpected purchaser of wool, considering the technological nature of modern warfare, is the US Army. Wool is used in the US military for berets and blankets but there are plans afoot to introduce woollen underwear. Not only would this mean greater comfort for the troops, through a range of different temperatures in theatres of operation, wool has advantages over manmade fibres, which are inclined to melt and cause horrific burns in combat situations.

A bi-product of woollen production that remains crucially important across the world is that of lanolin. Lanolin, a greasy substance that protects the wool whilst it is still on the back of the sheep is a complex mixture of chemicals known as esters, together with alcohol and fatty acids. Lanolin is removed from wool during the scouring process and is then purified. It is one of the most versatile bi-products imaginable and is used amongst other things in adhesive tape and in printing inks. It is also added to motor oil and is present in many lubricants. Lanolin is also crucial to the cosmetics industry and is an invaluable ingredient in lipstick, eye shadow, mascara, shampoos and hair conditioners. Many skin creams and lotions are lanolin based because the grease produced by our woolly mammal cousins rarely causes irritation or allergic response.

Research in New Zealand has recently led to some startling conclusions about the uses and quality of dairy products obtained from sheep. It appears that people who maintain a fat-rich diet and who are in danger from increased cholesterol are safer using milk and cheese from sheep. Partly as a result of this research consumption of sheep dairy products is growing massively in developed countries, though there is nothing remotely new about it. In order, the world's leaders in the production of sheep's milk are Turkey, Italy, Greece, Syria and Rumania. Across the world sheep-derived protein is crucial to the survival and health of hundreds of millions of people. Many sheep breeders are now looking for a strain of sheep that provides good quality fleece, milk for cheese and yoghurt and which also produces hides and mutton. Taken together, these advantages mean that the sheep remains by far and away the most versatile and useful animal in sustainable farming. What is more, there are breeds of sheep that can provide all these benefits, whilst at the same time being able to survive in circumstances that would spell death to pigs or cattle.

No matter how important sheep may remain across the world today, it is their role in history up to this point in time that really sets them apart. Without sheep, hunter-gatherers may never have become pastoralists or farmers. Human populations would have remained small and human advancement would have been very limited. The first true civilizations were made possible by the domestication of sheep and remained utterly dependent on them. As a result sheep have become deeply enshrined in myth, folklore and religion around the planet.

The seeds of the truly modern world were planted in 12th-century Europe, when a trade in sheep's wool and finished cloth was deliberately fostered. This was most notable in the case of religious groups such as the Cistercians and the Knights Templar, who by their efforts broke the bonds of feudal isolation and introduced the basis of what would become genuine world trade. Affluent people living in Central and Western Europe increasingly sought luxury goods, only obtainable from the East. Wool provided the basic commodity that allowed markets to develop in places such as Champagne. The Champagne fairs represented the staging post from local barter to international trade and they also introduced the mechanisms of credit and speculation upon which international markets still depend. They were only the first of many such fairs but they represented a crucial benchmark.

It was the wool-millionaires of Italy who began to spend their excess wealth on art, architecture, scientific investigation and education. They also founded banks that would never have existed but for wool and the cloth made from it. Wealth derived from the woollen trade built the first Italian universities and introduced experiments in democracy and rational-thinking, the results of which would flow out across Europe as the Renaissance gained pace. Enlightenment led to a distrust of religious leadership and ultimately spelled the end of the Roman Catholic Church as a powerful adjunct to feudal repression. New Christian denominations were the result – the adherents of which began to develop a different view of life and individuality. This led to a new view of personal advancement and achievement enshrined in what was known as the Protestant Ethic.

Voyages of discovery, many of which also owed their possibility to wealth derived from wool, began to open up the world. As a result Europeans came upon not one but two new continents to the west. With the first European settlers came sheep, which were soon integrated into the lives of indigenous Americans. With such prosperous new colonies ripe for the picking, the more powerful maritime nations of Europe began to vie for control of both continents and the age of modern imperialism dawned. Religious wars were rife all over Europe and these ultimately led to the demise of Spain, Portugal and Holland as leading world nations. France and Britain alone retained sufficient wealth and power to exploit both the Americas and other regions of the world opened up by exploration.

In Britain, everything was changing rapidly during the 18th century. Old methods of farming were giving way to new techniques. These meant more abundant crops and a massive increase in efficiency. But at the same time the sheep was certainly not forgotten. On the contrary, the old manorial system gave way more and more to large enclosed areas of land, many of which were given over to intensive sheep rearing. Whole communities were wiped out, especially in Scotland and Ireland, and replaced by massive herds of sheep, bred for profit to feed the rapacious appetite of the growing woollen textile industry, especially in England.

For hundreds of years a break-even point had been established between those people necessary to spin wool and the people employed to weave it into cloth. The ratio was four people using spinning wheels to furnish the necessary yarn for one handloom. The invention of the Flying Shuttle by John Kay in 1733 may well represent the most important technological achievement in history. It was much faster than a handloom and it meant that to keep each weaver supplied with yarn would take sixteen spinners, working flat out. The only response possible was the creation of newer and much more efficient spinning machines, the first of which was the Spinning Jenny. The flying shuttle began an evolutionary process in machine development so that each part of the spinning, weaving and finishing of woollen textiles could keep pace. These machines, allied to waterpower, spelled industrialisation.

The whole of Great Britain turned itself into one large factory, a feat it achieved in an astonishingly short period of time. Different areas became known for specific skills and commodities, and all dedicated to driving forward the aims of industrialisation on a massive scale. The steam engine appeared, speeding up processes still further, burning thousands of tons of coal and made of iron – themselves incentives for other areas of Britain to get busy.

Again, originally because of wool, colonists in North America became discontented with British rule and fought to achieve their independence. They became adept at growing cotton, which was shipped to Britain and replaced wool as the 'in' fabric. It formed the backbone of the industrial boom of the 19th century. Everywhere people were being sucked into the towns from the countryside. The once crowded slopes of the lower Pennines became peaceful sheep granges, whilst the looms clattered ceaselessly in the mill towns. White hot metal spluttered in the iron works as new machines were produced, miners struggled underground to rip tin, copper and iron from the bowels of the earth, all to feed the rapacious appetite of something the world had never seen before – industrialisation on a massive scale.

With the wealth created Britain had the means to beat its old adversary France, which had been so ravaged by war and political uncertainty it failed to keep up with the racing technology. Virtually unopposed on the high seas for a crucial period Britain built a massive empire, the greatest the world had ever known. Working with the same principles that had originated in the Champagne fairs of France, great banking institutions came into being. Stocks and shares became commonplace – fortunes were made and lost and in the cramped, dirty, unhealthy conditions of the towns and cities, social welfare gradually became an issue, as both Britain and other nations clawed their way to eventual democracy.

The British industrial model was copied and often bettered by other nations. The sad inevitability was a striving for power and empire. This ultimately led to not one but two world wars, constantly changing the map of Europe, destroying age-old nation states and creating new ones in their place.

Today, in the early years of the 21st century, it sometimes seems as if we have learned very little. The world is replete with inequality. In the boom economies things have never been better. Life expectancy in Europe, the US and parts of Asia has never been so long in the history of the world as it is today. People generally enjoy an affluent lifestyle and have sufficient money to eat themselves into obesity. An avaricious consumer society gobbles up the world's resources at an unprecedented pace, whilst less developed cultures are peopled by individuals who still endure the same sort of misery that typified the worst examples of life in the early industrial cities.

Nevertheless, there is promise for the future. In the Far East, economies are booming, offering many millions a lifestyle they could not have contemplated only a short time ago. Much more could be done to help Third World countries, but there are signs that the developed world is at last starting to take note and to share at least a little of its wealth with those who still have so little.

So advanced has technology become that within the last half century we have broken the bounds, not only of nation states, but of the very Earth itself. Men have walked on the moon and they are set to travel to Mars, which will be the first stepping stone to who knows what destiny out amongst the stars.

From first to last, generations of sheep have patiently munched away at desert scrubland and lush grass pastures across virtually the entire surface of the planet. A billion of them are presently eating away as I write these words. Their basic need, like that of any species, is to survive and flourish. By forming this most essential symbiotic relationship with humanity, the sheep has moved from being a thinly dispersed wild animal of no special account to being perhaps the second most successful mammal on the Earth. Sheep didn't have much choice in the matter – they were a bi-product of the rise of humanity but what a fantastically important component they have been.

Perhaps we should look more carefully at these 'clouds with legs' that dot the valleys and hillsides of our planet. Maybe we should pause to think about the billions of them that have given their wool, and their bodies, so that we could leave behind a life of brutish uncertainty and reach for the stars. Human beings are ingenious and who knows, we might have managed to reach our present state even without the presence of the sheep, perhaps relying on other species to a greater extent. What would the world be like today if we had no sheep and would we ever have achieved nearly so much? But as I was constantly told when I was a child: 'if ifs and ands were pots and pans we'd have no need for metal'.

I propose a toast to the sheep – the most underrated and yet most important companion on our long and fascinating journey from a stark, cold and dismal cave to heaven knows where!

Index

O

is a symbol of the world,
of oneness and unity. O Books
explores the many paths of whole-
ness and spiritual understanding which
different traditions have developed down
the ages. It aims to bring this knowledge in
accessible form, to a general readership, pro-
viding practical spirituality to today's seekers.

For the full list of over 200 titles covering:
ACADEMIC/THEOLOGY • ANGELS • ASTROLOGY/
NUMEROLOGY • BIOGRAPHY/AUTOBIOGRAPHY
• BUDDHISM/ENLIGHTENMENT • BUSINESS/LEADERSHIP/
WISDOM • CELTIC/DRUID/PAGAN • CHANNELLING
• CHRISTIANITY; EARLY • CHRISTIANITY; TRADITIONAL
• CHRISTIANITY; PROGRESSIVE • CHRISTIANITY;
DEVOTIONAL • CHILDREN'S SPIRITUALITY • CHILDREN'S
BIBLE STORIES • CHILDREN'S BOARD/NOVELTY • CREATIVE
SPIRITUALITY • CURRENT AFFAIRS/RELIGIOUS • ECONOMY/
POLITICS/SUSTAINABILITY • ENVIRONMENT/EARTH
• FICTION • GODDESS/FEMININE • HEALTH/FITNESS
• HEALING/REIKI • HINDUISM/ADVAITA/VEDANTA
• HISTORY/ARCHAEOLOGY • HOLISTIC SPIRITUALITY
• INTERFAITH/ECUMENICAL • ISLAM/SUFISM
• JUDAISM/CHRISTIANITY • MEDITATION/PRAYER
• MYSTERY/PARANORMAL • MYSTICISM • MYTHS
• POETRY • RELATIONSHIPS/LOVE • RELIGION/
PHILOSOPHY • SCHOOL TITLES • SCIENCE/
RELIGION • SELF-HELP/PSYCHOLOGY
• SPIRITUAL SEARCH • WORLD
RELIGIONS/SCRIPTURES • YOGA

**Please visit our website,
www.O-books.net**